Tea, Rum & Fags

TEA, RUM & FAGS

SUSTAINING TOMMY 1914–18

ALAN WEEKS

The History Press

Cover illustrations: (front) Lancashire Fusiliers being dished out with stew from a dixie, March 1917 (reproduced by kind permission of the Imperial War Museum, Q.4843); (back) cooking on a scrounged stove, near Ovillers, July 1916 (reproduced by kind permission of the Imperial War Museum, Q.3993)

First published 2009

The History Press
The Mill, Brimscombe Port
Stroud, Gloucestershire, GL5 2QG
www.thehistorypress.co.uk

© Alan Weeks, 2009

British Library Cataloguing in Publication Data.
A catalogue record for this book is available from the British Library.

ISBN 978 0 7524 5000 1

Printed in Great Britain

Contents

One

Introduction – 'Mutinous Mutterings'

If Tommy Atkins was not getting as much tea as he wanted in the trenches, the rum ration had not arrived and he was short of cigarettes and eating little else but bully beef and hard biscuits, he was inclined to, as Private George Coppard put it, 'mutinous mutterings'. However, there was a positive side to this: having a grouse was considered good for morale. Captain Rowland Fielding of the 3rd Battalion of the Coldstream Guards noted that it was 'etiquette' for men to grumble, almost a cultural requirement.

Private Cuthill of the 4th Battalion Black Watch (4/Black Watch) wondered how 'they had the hard neck to say that the British Expeditionary Force [BEF] was the best fed Army in the world. Heaven help the worst fed army, then.' He reported that he was getting one slice of bread a day along with plenty of hard toil in the trench. Private Richard Beasley complained that he lived on tea and dog biscuits. He was lucky to get meat once a week. In addition, he asked his readers to try and imagine standing in a trench full of water with the smell of dead bodies nearby (the live ones stank pretty badly, too).

It was traditional for Tommy to have a moan (he never called himself 'Tommy' except by way of derision). The 'Old Contemptibles' of 1914, the old soldiers who made up the original BEF, were described by Captain Ritchie of the Cameron Highlanders as calm and unexcitable as long as there was plenty of sleep, food and rum. It was the lack of any of these which upset their customary affability. In the frequently cold and wet trenches a meal or a drink was something to look forward to, a comforting and sustaining event in an otherwise terrifying and miserable existence.

It was not only the occasional absence and shortage of food which raised Tommy's ire but also its monotony and the fact that it was sometimes uncooked or not as hot as it should be. Private W. Carson of the Hull Commercials hated the eternal sameness of bully beef and hard biscuits, and tea tasting of onions because it was brewed in the same container as the stew.

In 1914 and, for some battalions, a great deal of 1915, cooks were not even in the support areas just behind the front line but kept back in rest areas miles to the rear. When they did arrive in 1915 and thereafter they were not often in front-line trenches but in the reserve areas and the transport lines. Cooked food had to come up along communication trenches or tracks usually about half a mile long, and the ration parties carrying it up at night could take hours to arrive because of enemy action, damage to the trench and the weather conditions, not to mention the dark (see Chapter Five).

Until insulated containers were used later in the war the food arrived lukewarm at best, and even these 'hay boxes' could be rendered ineffective by delays, accidents and cold weather. Tommy continued to complain that the best way to ensure that food was hot was to have the cooks in the trench with him. In these circumstances, many soldiers collected a whole array of cooking devices (described in Chapter Six) to cook or warm up what food they had and, most importantly, to brew tea.

Another common grievance was that food could be depleted due to pilfering on its way up to the front. The 'devils' in this were Army Service Corps (ASC) personnel and drivers, who had a reputation for dealing in an enormous black market of stolen ration goods. They tended not to steal bully beef and hard biscuits – explaining why the Poor Bloody Infantry got so much of them in relation to other food which was easier to sell on the black market. Other suspects were the cooks themselves and their mates, NCOs and even the ration parties who were supposed to be delivering all the food to their company.

In the thick of dreadful battles like the Somme a lot depended on sustaining Tommy. According to 2nd Lieutenant Charles Edmonds it was the basics which concerned the troops most of all – enough bully beef and biscuits (no matter how fed up he was with them), tea, rum and fags. If Tommy got them he wouldn't feel so bad, although he also liked a bit of fried bacon for his breakfast, some 'dog and maggot' (biscuit and cheese) for his dinner, and 'rooty' and 'pozzy' (bread and jam) for his tea.

The bully beef might be of poor quality, as well. The Fray Bentos product was good but other makes were very dry and too full of gristle, fat and ground-up bone. Tommy might also receive a 'Maconochie' – tinned dried meat and vegetables (M and V) but this could be a greasy hash with not a lot of any known meat. Tins of 'pork' and beans were notoriously short of meat. Dodgy profiteers made fortunes in the war supplying inferior food for inflated prices, such as jam made with marrows.

There were often justifiable excuses for the non-arrival of food in the trenches, not least enemy shelling and bombing which damaged roads and railways, lorries and trains, and the communication trenches and tracks. Cold and wet weather could also make life very difficult for those trying to bring up the grub. The winters of 1916/17 and 1917/18 were especially bad. Rainfall in August 1917 in Flanders was 127mm, the average for August being 70mm. When the Battle of Arras began in April 1917 it was still snowing.

Distances from the English ports to the front lines were relatively short – Londoners heard the bombardments on the Somme and the mining of Messines Ridge. Moreover, for a large part of the war the front lines were relatively static. For these two substantial reasons Tommy may have good cause to complain when the 'scran' failed to turn up. However, from the point of view of those working hard to organise and sustain methods and routes of supply there were many mitigating circumstances. At its largest in December 1917 the BEF numbered 2,077,000 men, of whom 1,250,000 were combatants. To get daily rations to this many soldiers in battle areas was a logistical nightmare demanding the complex employment of a fair proportion of the 827,000 who were not in the front line. This system only significantly broke down at the sharp end when the BEF was in rapid retreat in 1914 and 1918 (Chapter Thirteen). There were more local difficulties during the big British offensives, notably the Somme in 1916 and Flanders in 1917 (Chapter Nine), and the rapid advance in 1918, and when individual units were moving to and from the front line (Chapter Fourteen).

Another perspective on the 'mutinous mutterings' is to emphasise that they referred generally to the lack of food and drink in the trenches. When soldiers were back in the rest areas they not only had a good chance of getting all their rations but there were also numerous Army and other canteens and civilian establishments to provide extras.

However, pay of a shilling a day tended to limit use of these places so they could have a good mutter about this, especially if there were no parcels from home.

So how much of the time was Tommy in the trenches? Charles Carrington provided a useful profile of this with his analysis for the 7/ Royal Sussex. This battalion spent forty-two per cent of 1915–1918 in front-line or support trenches. Carrington also calculated he spent sixty-five days of 1916 in front line trenches, about a sixth of the year.

Another revealing point from Carrington was that he described most of the recruits to his battalion as skinny, sallow, shambling and nervous victims of an industrial system. Wartime shortages of food at home had made them even poorer specimens. Carrington recorded that after six months of regular nourishment, fresh air and hard physical work they looked twice as big as they did when they arrived. In fact, they were officially measured and weighed: their average development in six months was an extra inch in height and a stone in weight. An anxious mother wrote to Carrington complaining that her Johnny was half-starved. Johnny, in fact, had grown two inches and was two stones heavier. My father volunteered in the spring of 1917 (he was in a reserved occupation – docker) largely because he was half-starved. He weighed nine stone. When he left Cologne in November 1919 he weighed thirteen and a half stone.

Indeed, when Tommy got his full tot of rum early in the morning and there was bacon to fry and bully beef stew to follow for dinner and countless cups of 'sergeant-major' (very strong, very sweet) tea and plenty of cigarettes he wouldn't grumble too much. Alfred McLelland Burrage, a short story writer in civvy street but in the Artists' Rifles in 1917, described his pals as 'perambulating stomachs'. Reasonable food and drink and cigarettes helped Tommy to endure the worst days in the trenches, whilst he could look forward to egg and chips and 'van blong' in a nice, warm *estaminet*, sitting in a chair and eating at a table, hopefully served by a pretty girl.

Two

Bully Beef and Hard Biscuits

A Tramway Accident for Meat

'Boeuf bouilli' had a Napoleonic origin but in 1914 'bully beef' was re-translated by French urchins, hoping to persuade Tommies to hand over a tin or two of it, as 'boolee biff'. It had been used by the British Army from about the 1860s. It formed a fundamental basis of trench diet and continued to be served up in the back areas. Songs and poems were composed about it. Lieutenant W.S. Dane's *My Bully Beef* described it as a 'tramway accident for meat' and deplored its repeated delivery for breakfast, dinner, tea and supper.

In common with the rest of the 4/Seaforth Highlanders and nearly all the infantry he was fed up with the stuff. But, if famished, Dane considered each bite a joy. He was probably being sarcastic, although the type produced by Fray Bentos was acceptable. Less popular brands could be really dreadful. Edmund Blunden remembered befriending a stray terrier in the trenches, but when he tried to feed it with W.H. Davies's bully beef it wisely cleared off.

Lieutenant Dane suggested in his last verse that if he were killed he would probably be ground up and served as bully beef. Indeed, an ugly rumour went the rounds of the Western Front that German 'Rindfleish' was of human origin. That certainly was the verdict of men of 2/West Yorkshire who discovered some tins of it in a captured trench in November 1916.

Calories

It was mostly the sheer monotony of a diet of bully beef and hard biscuits which depressed the front-line infantry, even if it was reasonably
hot in a stew. But how did it fare in terms of nutritional value or calories? The official daily ration prescribed in 1914 was 4,193 calories. The
detailed analysis of this in Chapter Seven tends to the view that the
experts underestimated the amount of hard physical work the infantry
had to undertake in the trenches. They had to carry rations to the front
trenches, ammunition, equipment and other supplies under the cover
of darkness. The construction, maintenance and repair of earthworks
and wire entanglements were round-the-clock jobs, not to mention the
small business of actually fighting and keeping an eye on the enemy.

The ration made provision for the substitution of fresh or frozen meat
and bread by preserved meat and hard biscuits. In terms of nutrition the
schedule provided 4,279 calories with fresh or frozen meat and bread
but 4,625 with preserved meat and hard biscuits. A daily calorie count of
1,653 for hard biscuits meant that it was quite tempting to keep supplying this carbohydrate-high food in order to claim that the daily ration
was being met. The preserved meat/biscuit diet, in fact, if not satisfying
and morale-boosting, was scientifically sound.

This remained the case in 1917 when reductions in the schedule for
meat and bread produced a calorie count of only 3,665. In fact, the
preserved meat ration was maintained and the biscuit one only slightly
reduced, producing a calorie count of 4,349, which was still above the
official daily ration. So, by this time, there was even more of a temptation to concentrate on sending up bully beef and biscuits because the
U-boat campaign had created serious fresh food shortages and rationing
in Britain.

Maconochie and Pork and Beans

Preserved meat supplies could be tins of 'Maconochie' or pork and
beans. Some battalions did quite well with these and it relieved the
monotony of bully and biscuits. Others rarely saw either which made
the culinary tedium worse for them. Cecil Withers of 17/Royal Fusiliers
got Maconochie about once a month.

Maconochie was variously described as a sort of Irish stew in tins, or a beef stew with potato and mixed vegetables, or, succinctly, a dinner in a tin. In fact, this was George Coppard's favourite meal as long as it was heated (cold, it was not so palatable). The original beef and vegetable tin was made by Maconochie Bros. of London. They claimed on the tin that the meat was prepared with all its natural juices with no extracts used. The company had won 143 gold medals and the highest awards. Testimonials to the quality of this food appeared in *The Wipers Times*: Corporal 'Will Bashem' proposed to call on Mr Maconochie on his next leave to personally thank him. Trooper 'Smiler' Marshall of the Essex Yoemanry wrote that James William Maconochie made a monarchy on his own with beans mixed up with turnips and carrots and all sorts of things ('the troops did a funny'un when an onion came to light').

The tin produced by Moir Wilson was also highly regarded. But, unfortunately, there were many inferior brands which it was unwise to eat in the dark. One contained a piece of rotten meat and some boiled rice. Some ran with liquid or were like a grisly hash.

Sometimes Maconochie was really scarce generally. Working at the St Jean Casualty Clearing Station near Ypres in December 1917 my father regarded it as a luxury, so when an RAMC corporal delivered a carton of ten tins, George was a very happy man.

Others had far too much of the stuff, and gluts like this usually meant that a lot of the rubbish Maconochie was being used. It could be powerful: a group in the 2/Field Company, Royal Engineers had the habit of hiding their tinned treasures in a home-made stove. They arrived back late to their billet in Fonquevillers one night and lit the stove, forgetting that the Maconochie was inside. The resulting explosion ripped out the sides of the flimsy stove (it was just an old dixie with holes punched in it). They really got their M and V hot that night.

Digging M and V cold out of the tin with a jack knife was not very satisfying, unless you were really starving. It was cooked in its tin to conserve fuel and how more men did not go down with tin or lead poisoning is a mystery. Perhaps their stomachs were already hardened by all the mud, sand and sandbag hairs they already swallowed with their food, not to mention what was in the tea.

Tins of pork and beans exhibited the same sort of varying quality. American brands were good but in some products Tommy was lucky to find any sort of pork and, if he did, it could be a little lump of fat hidden amongst the beans, another example of profiteering back home.

Lieutenant Tyndale-Biscoe complained to his HQ about this and received a reply suggesting that troops should not be disappointed if there appeared to be no pork in tins of pork and beans. This was simply a matter of the pork being absorbed into the beans. 'In that case,' replied Tyndale-Biscoe, 'why not just send "meat lozenges"?'

Iron Rations

Not only was bully beef a solid part of daily rations, it also made up the bulk of emergency rations carried by the infantry in case food supplies dried up completely for some reason. These were 'iron rations' – also slang for hails of German shells at dawn. Lieutenant J.B. MacLean of 1/Cameronians described the package containing these iron rations as resembling a horse's feed bag. It usually contained a twelve-ounce tin of bully beef (bigger one and a half or seven-pound tins were used for normal rations), hard biscuits, tea and sugar. In some bags there was a piece of cheese or a cube of meat extract.

Sometimes the tea and sugar were already mixed in a tin. Sometimes there was only tea. There was seldom any condensed milk so the sort of tea they would have to drink in an emergency would not have been palatable to the men. They carried two pints of water in a bottle on the right hip. This may not have been enough to make much tea and in conditions of advance or retreat there may not have been time to brew it up. The 2/Cameronians aimed to carry two days' water supply on the Armentières Front in August 1915.

The troops were not allowed to start on their iron rations without an officer's permission. Tom MacDonald of the 9/Royal Sussex asked his platoon commander when he could eat them. The answer was trenchant: 'You can start on them when your belly button hits your backbone and your hip bones stick out of your trousers.'

There were occasions when the emergency rations had to be consumed because there was nothing else. This was common during the headlong retreats of 1914 and 1918 and in the big British offensives such as the Somme. The 1/1/Monmouths, including Private Dick Trafford, ate cheese and hard biscuits for several days in November 1916, and the London Rifle Brigade ate iron rations from 21–27 November 1917. Eventually they ran out of bully beef and existed on biscuits and contaminated water from the open trenches of shell holes which characterised this stage of the Third Battle of Ypres (Passchendaele).

Many troops never ate iron rations. Charles Carrington ordered it only once in three years and that was when marching away from the front after a few difficult days. Sometimes rats ate them, a fate suffered by the package belonging to Private Andrew Bowie of the 1/Cameronians in August 1917.

Stew

If there was nothing else but bully beef and biscuits at least it was a meal, and because of the calorie count it made men feel full up. Any meal was an oasis of pleasure in an otherwise dreadful day. It provided an opportunity to gather round a stove or a little fire (sometimes forbidden because of tell-tale smoke) and have a laugh and a joke.

There were ways of making bully beef more palatable. It could be fried with onions or crumbled with hard biscuit to make a hot hash. With vegetables (sometimes dried in packets) added all this could make a tasty stew, vastly superior to just digging a knife into a cold tin. When cooks came up to the transport lines they sent up stews like this in dixies – two-gallon iron containers. Tommy could cook some himself for a bit extra using Tommy Cookers, spirit cookers or improvised stoves, and using mess tins as pots or pans.

A hot stew was particularly satisfying after days of cold food. It could vary in quality – just like the cooks. At least if the Tommies stewed it themselves they probably knew what was in it. Private Mervyn Rees of the Royal Honourable Artillery remembered the bliss of hot stew at 4am on the morning of 7 December 1914, when he was soaked to the skin with little prospect of getting any drier. But Lieutenant Vaughan (1/8/Royal Warwicks) had a different experience of a lukewarm, greasy liquid in which floated half-cooked pieces of meat and shreds of sorry-looking cabbage. At least there was jam pudding to follow.

Men of the 7/Queen's Own West Kents also recalled little bits of unhealthy-looking meat floating in some sad liquid. Tommy finished up getting too much stew (and also pea soup, another favourite and easy way of meeting the vegetable ration), because cutting up fresh or frozen meat and slinging it in a stewing pot was the simplest way to get it up to the trenches. There was a popular saying in 1917: if the sun rises in the East it is a sure sign there will be stew for dinner. 'Eternal stew', Winston Groom called it.

Tins – Full and Empty

The monotony of the diet is attested to by the litter of tins in No Man's Land and disused trenches and saps. Lieutenant Pitt of the Border Regiment counted them in their thousands over a few square yards. Smiler Marshall reckoned it was a good way of tempting rats out of the trenches: the idea was to throw them (tins and rats) as far as you could. Many tins became entangled in the outer lines of barbed wire creating a strange cacophony of sound at night as the breezes moved them around.

The big seven-pound tins of bully beef came in handy as improvised stoves or chamber pots. A few men shot themselves in the foot through full bully beef tins in order to make a reasonable mess of it without blowing the appendage off or creating tell-tale powder burns around the wound; the hope was to get sent to hospital in Britain (a 'Blighty One'). On the other hand, they could be court-martialled for a Self-Inflicted Wound (SIW). Robert Lothian Ramsay of the Black Watch was sheltering behind a haystack at the Battle of Loos (September 1915) when a bullet struck his emergency ration pack. This took most of the impact out of the missile and he got a Blighty One to Stobswell Hospital. Discerning Tommies discovered that early symptoms of trench fever could be accelerated by consuming large quantities of bully beef and biscuits, getting you out of the trench sooner rather than later.

Even in August 1914, at the very start of the war, Private Ernest Parker (10/Durham Light Infantry) recalled that French children soon realised that the food most likely to be given away by the Tommies was tins of bully beef and hard biscuits, hence their cries for 'Boolee biff' and 'biskwi' (followed by volleys of English obscenities – they learnt very quickly – if they didn't get anything). Full tins of wasted bully beef were sometimes used to make the trench floor and support the walls, parapet and parados (rear bank). This was recorded as early as January 1915. Captain Gerald Burgoyne remembered seeing enough full bully beef tins to feed a battalion thrown away in Kemmel near

Ypres because tinned salmon was available in this sector. There were thousands of full hard biscuit tins also discarded when fresh bread was available. Actually, they made very good fuel for fires. Burgoyne also spotted an artillery HQ where the tent floors and the paths were made entirely of full tins of bully beef. My father told me they made very good foot scrapers.

Men who were sentenced to field punishments because of misdemeanours had to live on bully beef and biscuits for seven to twenty-eight days, and received no pay. Subsisting on this diet caused constipation. Being tied to a wagon wheel for several hours a day was bad enough but simultaneously enduring digestive pains added to the suffering.

Dog Biscuits

The Army Biscuit – Huntley and Palmer's No. 4 (although my father was eating 'No. Fives' in 1917) was commonly referred to as a 'dog biscuit'. It was so hard that men with false teeth suffered badly. They were also a danger to perfectly healthy molars. They could be soaked in water to soften them, or broken up with some hefty blows from a trenching tool handle or any large stone, and crumbled to put in a stew. Private Pressey of the Royal Artillery tried to smash one with the corner of a brick but hit his hand instead. When he did manage to break it up he soaked the fragments in water for several days. He then heated and drained the hash, poured condensed milk over it and ate the lot. These whole-wheat biscuits were about four inches square and half an inch thick. They were so hard that John Osborne (4/Devons) was able to cut the middle out of one and stick a photograph of his mother in it.

No surprise, then, that dog biscuits were often referred to as 'those f★★★★★★ biscuits', especially by Private Pressey. This led the chaplain of the 2/Royal Welsh Fusiliers to try and persuade his commanding officer (CO) to put a guard outside the battalion canteen in case any biscuit attempted an act of indecency (Suzanne, 2 February 1917). They were often slung out into No Man's Land in disgust and Harry Patch vividly remembered two dogs fighting over a pile of them.

Despite Tommy's general low regard for bully beef and biscuits it was his staple diet and without it he would have found it almost impossible to endure the hardships and terrors of the trenches. What other

An evening out in Berles-au-Bois, September 1915. Drawing by Les Read.

inexpensive foods could have been eaten cold and carried about in tins? He knew he was eating real meat, even if it was accompanied by gristle, fat and bone. With Maconochie the amount of meat could vary enormously, and some of that could also be gristle, fat and bone. Tins of 'pork' and beans could also let the soldier down. But bully beef made a good, hot stew and eating a few biscuits could cram Tommy's stomach with carbohydrates.

Three

Tea and Rum

'Sergeant-Major' Tea

Tea had to be hot, strong and heavily sweetened with sugar and condensed milk ('sergeant-major' tea – in the sense that the CSM would always get the best of anything) in order to sustain the soldier through the day and the night – mug after mug of the stuff. It must have been very comforting to have the hot, brown, nectar-like brew steaming in a mug near your elbow.

Tea, indeed, worked wonders. During the First Battle of Ypres on the last day of October 1914 the CO of the 2/Royal Welsh Fusiliers arrived at an artillery battery in a terrible state after the action at Gheluvelt. But when Lieutenant Ralph Blewitt handed him a mug of tea, with a fag and a slice of bread and jam, he was a rejuvenated man.

Frank Dunham, as a stretcher-bearer on the Somme in November 1916, soon learnt that the moment he got a wounded man back to safety his duty was to hand him some tea and help him to drink it if necessary. Men of the 2/West Yorkshires in the same month shouted, 'Get a drop of tea for Fritz', even though the poor blighter, badly wounded, would probably have preferred coffee with Schnapps in it.

'Tea up! Char! Jildy!' was the shout from the ration orderlies as they arrived with the blackened dixies full of hot tea. The first mug of the day was 'gunfire tea' – a salute to standing down from night duty. Men ran from all parts of the trench with outstretched mugs. Of course, the efforts of cooks in transport lines and ration parties could not produce enough tea. The Tommies had to brew, or 'drum up', some of their own.

'Tommy Cookers' could be very useful here because these little tins of solid fuel were smokeless. Smoke was sometimes banned because it invited enemy artillery fire. However, some Tommies became experts at building tiny and virtually smokeless fires. NCOs also might turn a blind eye to a fire, especially if they got some tea out of it. It was slow going on the Tommy Cooker: in one estimate (possibly pessimistic), they took two hours to boil half a pint of water, which made it difficult to keep up with the demand for tea. Luckily, most of the time, bigger stoves were in use, boiling large pots or tins of water.

The tea ration was meant to provide six pints of tea a day, which was not enough for Tommy, and so this had to be supplemented by purchases from canteens and the contents of parcels from home. Anyone a bit short on tea would get help from his pals.

Even if stoves were in use there were frequent problems of getting enough fuel for the fires. Rations of coal, coke or charcoal were not enough or infrequent so there were searches for wood. This sometimes meant that trench-floor duckboards, 'A' frames from the bottom and sides, trench revetting, and even assault ladders, disappeared. NCOs once again had to turn blind eyes if they wanted some extra tea, although there was a lot of bravado from thirsty men – 'They haven't got our range yet, Sarn't!' (referring to the warning that the enemy artillery might spot their smoke), or 'They're too busy doing their own drumming up, Sarn't'. Ernest Parker and other members of 10/Durham Light Infantry – feisty soldiers – simply ignored an order not to light up (Menin Road, 14 September 1915).

Their own brew would definitely be of the sergeant-major variety. Cecil Withers complained about the stuff coming up from the cooks – 'What they call "tea"!' It needed to have a toffee-like consistency. The cooks were badgered to put in extra tins of the syrupy condensed milk. The amount of caffeine and tannin consumed by Tommies probably helped to keep them awake during the night watch. The downside must have been the frequency of urinating, which was why empty tins and German *pickelhaube* helmets came in so handy.

The Taste of Tea

Lots of sugar and condensed milk were not the only ingredients in the tea: other less desirable elements also found their way in. In the first place

Tommy had to get used to the grease and scum from the cooking pots and dixies or insulated containers, because all the stews were cooked or poured into them as well as the tea. Even if you made your own there were still the other contaminants to contend with. All the water was conveyed in ex-petrol tins so any tea habitually tasted of petrol. Stored water was also treated with chloride of lime to guard against disease.

Trenches were sometimes surrounded by shell holes containing water so it was possible to crawl out at night and collect some. The trouble was that it was never certain what was in this water. It could taste of gunpowder or there might be poison gas lurking about in the hollows. The crump holes could also hide other secrets. My father told me that he once drank blue tea made with water from a shell hole. Later on they saw a dead German floating in it. The corporal cook was unmoved: 'It's the live ones you have to worry about, George, mate,' he said. But George subsequently laid off the blue tea.

After months of drinking this stuff Tommy got used to petrol and chloride of lime in his beverage. It was a very good reason to shove in plenty of sugar and condensed milk. Machine-gun crews were at times accused of firing off a few rounds so that they could boil a pot on their hot gun: the tea tasted of machine oil. Similar to this was having a brew from hot train engines as they made one of their frequent stops, as Ernest Parker discovered to his benefit on his way to Poperinghe in August 1915.

The taste of tea also explained why there was a practice of putting your rum ration into it, especially when there was no condensed milk available. However, Tommies were hooked on very sweet tea and soon tired of the laced variety: the 2/Royal Welsh Fusiliers (RWF) complained about it during the First Battle of Ypres in 1914. Such was the attraction of condensed milk that some men actually drank it neat.

Officers liked a mixture of tea, rum and sugar – a 'posset'. Lieutenant Mottram shared this with his men near the Yser Canal opposite Brielen late in 1915, and his CO accused him of a gross breach of regimental 'etiquette'. Posset was not for Tommies, apparently.

Tea Behind the Lines

Tea consumption remained high in the rest areas but since van blong (or 'plonk') and beer were available, a continuous brew was not necessary.

But 'dry' (non-alcoholic) canteens were rated on the quality of their tea – how hot it was, strength and sweetness. Second Lieutenant John Glubb rated the tea in the YMCA huts as 'excellent'.

Tea also featured prominently in the offerings of Talbot House in Poperinghe, the origin of the Toc H movement and a haven for war-weary men. Daily tea in the chaplain's room (Talbot House was 'dry') was a very popular event. Tommy could write his letter home, mug at hand, in civilised surroundings. Or there was tea in the garden, a real delight on nice days, or in the canteen or in the special tea bar. Tea, in fact, was the tops in Talbot House. No wonder 5,000 men a week entered its portals; 117 were counted in ten minutes on one day.

The Rosy Glow of Rum

'Up spirits' was the cry at dawn when the rum ('Tom Thumb') arrived. 'Good health, sir', they muttered at the officer as they poured it down their throats. It certainly did lift spirits. Ernest Parker at St Julien in December 1915 described how the rosy glow of the strong, black spirit crept slowly like fire down to his feet. It was a major event of the day. Tommy could actually smell it as the officer or NCO with the earthenware jar approached round the corner. The aroma as the lid came off was intoxicating. It was a cheery occasion on cheerless days, the cue for much ribald humour and banter.

Lieutenant-Colonel Frank Crozier of the 9/Royal Irish Rifles described rum as a medicine, a temporary restorative in times of great stress. It certainly raised the fighting spirit of some soldiers. Private Ted Francis of the 16/Royal Warwicks remembered how rum made him feel nothing would hurt him – 'Right! Where's Jerry – up and at 'em!' Mind you, on this occasion Francis had managed to procure half a glassful of the stuff, an unusually generous dose: the normal measure was about an egg cupful.

Lieutenant-Colonel Jack declared that rum was not a 'battle dope'. In the bitterly cold days of January 1916 and January 1917 the rum ration simply warmed them up at the coldest time of the day. In the 1917 winter a practice grew of serving up the rum in the dead of night when it was even colder, as in the cases of the 1/Hull Pals and the 6/Welch. Sometimes there were double rations before men went over the top to give them Dutch Courage. It was also very handy for toothache or abscess pain.

There were extra tots for sentries coming off sentry duty or patrols or raid parties returning from No Man's Land at night, or during heavy bombardments. Private Pearson said it could blot out memories of the very recent past. In the view of Sergeant Harry Finch (7/Royal Sussex) a double ration for men waiting to go over the top during the night of 31 July 1917, the opening day of the Third Battle of Ypres, simply put them to sleep.

Getting Your Fair Share of Rum

There are conflicting accounts about the alcoholic strength of the rum. It was supposed to be forty per cent but the navy rum issued during the first few months of the war was reckoned to be stronger than that. John Reith said that men in his battalion in 1914 could not drink the rum neat but had to put it in their tea. This stronger rum ran out before the end of the year but even in 1918 Lieutenant Blacker of 4/Coldstream Guards made sure his men had plenty of hot tea in order to take down their rum. Soldiers of the 1/5/Royal Warwicks in 1916 said that their rum was so powerful it brought tears to their eyes.

The official ration was a quarter of a 'gill' or one-sixteenth of a pint. But this was seldom adhered to, so it seems. This measure was about four tablespoons, yet, in the event, it was often only two tablespoons, the measure John Reith mentioned in 1914. Corporal Charles Quinnell (9/Royal Fusiliers) remembered 'a big tablespoon' being used during the Second Battle of Ypres in April 1915. The 2/RWF were getting one and a half tablespoons in October 1914 and June 1915. Corporal Edward Glendinning (12/Sherwood Foresters), however, reckoned that he and his pals could drink as much as they liked at the Battle of Loos in September 1915.

Captain Billy Nevill issued an egg cupful, which was four table-spoons, the full ration, to his East Surrey men in October 1915. This battalion seemed to have done better than most because in August 1917 they were given 'half a mug' between five men, probably a quarter of a pint, slightly more than three tablespoons per man, still below the official ration. The 1/Cameronians had a double ration throughout

December 1914 – half a gill per man. Thereafter, there is no evidence of such largesse for them.

Second Lieutenant Charles Edmonds (5/Royal Warwicks) referred to a gallon jar for sixty-four men, equal to eight tablespoons per man, and so did John Brophy and Eric Partridge in *Dictionary of Tommies' Songs and Slang 1914–1918*. Winston Groom of the London Rifle Brigade received a 'dessert' spoonful at the end of 1915.

From these examples and exceptions, there is good reason to believe that the amount of rum actually received in the trenches was generally about half the official ration, which explained the infantry's craving for more of it. Private Pollard of the Honourable Royal Artillery recalled that he lived for the rum, which 'was all too meagre'. Winston Groom wanted twice as much twice as often.

Reductions gave rise to heightened if not vociferous 'mutterings'. The 2/RWF had their quota halved in January 1917 (one of the coldest months of the war). If only half the ration was being given out anyway, this reduced it to just a quarter of the ration. The Connaught Rangers had an issue only once every three days in December 1916 (also very cold).

Robert Graves was of the opinion that the sick parades of the 2/RWF rose alarmingly when the ration was cut or did not arrive. Like any other ration it was at the mercy of enemy action, the weather, damage to the communication trench, pilfering and the calibre and persistence of ration parties. Men in more isolated positions – artillery observers, snipers, signallers, machine-gun crews and the like – were even more likely to miss out on their rum. Sometimes they were simply forgotten.

Seldom Reaches Destination

The most bitter complaint of all was that men further back down the supply lines helped themselves to rum intended for front-line troops. There was some justification for the accusation of 'milking' if the ration was not forthcoming. And the depredations might have occurred nearer to the trenches. The popular song *Never Mind* suggested that 'the sergeant was entitled to a tot but not the bloody lot'. It was easy for anyone bringing up the rum jar to have a sly swig in the dark; ration party work was hard but there was always the chance of a bit of extra rum. In fairness to Tommy, however, he would normally consider his mates and leave the rum alone. There was no such reluctance to pinch the rum of other units. Black Jock MacMillan (1/Argyll and Sutherland Highlanders) stole the whole rum ration of a battalion (Middlesex) new to the trenches (16 March 1915).

'SRD' was printed on every jar – it stood for 'Special Rations Department', but according to popular opinion it meant 'Seldom Reaches Destination' or 'Soon Runs Dry' or 'Service Rum Diluted', another clever way to get a bit extra somewhere behind the trenches. Soldiers were always on the look-out for more rum to compensate for the 'leakages'. Someone in the 2/RWF got hold of an extra jar three-quarters full on 26 September 1915. NCOs were particularly adept at conjuring up extra jars, seemingly out of thin air.

'Open Up!'

When the ration reached the trench its distribution was supposed to take place in the presence of an officer. Either he or an NCO under his supervision put the tots in men's mouths, calling, 'Open up!' It took Billy Nevill two and a half hours to do this job but it gave him a chance to speak to each man. Other less efficient or caring officers might leave the job entirely to a senior NCO. For the 9/Royal Fusiliers during the Second Battle of Ypres in April 1915 each CSM issued four lots of rum to the four platoon sergeants, who did the actual doling out.

Lieutenant-Colonel Frank Crozier warned of the perils of this sort of practice. He was proved right in one case concerning the Loyal North Lancashires when a sergeant-major was left to distribute the rum. He obviously exceeded the correct dose, and had a fair bit himself, because when they went out on patrol to capture a surrounded group of Germans, for some incomprehensible reason he called out 'Fire' with the result that his men, in a circle, shot at each other. Other examples of drunkenness as a result of drinking excessive rum in the front line are described in Chapter Nineteen. There is no suggestion that these were more than isolated cases. Tommy looked forward to getting blind drunk when he was in the rest areas.

Relish

Private Henry Russell of the 5/London was lying badly wounded out in No Man's Land with little hope of being rescued. But he had with him a large bottle (originally containing Worcester Sauce or Yorkshire Relish) filled with rum and he decided to gulp down the lot in the hope of killing himself. But the only result of this colossal binge was to make him cheerful, and eventually sleepy. When he woke up he decided he wanted to live after all and managed to crawl back to where a stretcher-bearer could pick him up.

As indicated previously, rum could be diluted with water, but other substances were used to fill up rum jars which had been emptied by illicit drinking behind the lines. The London Rifle Brigade received one full of a powerful disinfectant ('Condy's Fluid'). One man drank some and died. There was nut oil or whale oil in others. Chinese labourers used whale oil to put on their feet. The QMS of the 2/RWF thought he had 'discovered' a jar of rum on 21 October 1914 only to discover that it contained creosote.

As the Germans retreated to the Hindenburg Line in the early months of 1917 they left some nasty booby traps, including a rum jar which exploded when it was uncorked by men of the 1/Grenadier Guards.

'No-rum' Divisions

Rum did not reach some Tommies because their divisional commander banned it, which they had powers to do even following medical advice on the effects of arduous conditions. If the general, in his wisdom, decided that rum was not good for Tommy, that was it. Religious groups in Britain campaigned against the issues led by Sir Victor Horsley. The 'no-rum' generals may have been swayed by these people, or they simply believed that rum impaired the efficiency of the troops. There was little general evidence that this was the case. When Siegfried Sassoon returned from sickness in 1917 he discovered that his divisional commander, Major-General Whincop, was a 'no-rum' man. So was Major-General Reginald Pinney.

A few lower-ranking officers also banned rum even in 'rum' divisions. A ration was given to the 2/RWF an hour before the attack at Loos on

25 September 1915 but one company commander had it poured away into the ground. He obviously thought it did the troops no good.

This could be a form of punishment, too. A platoon of the 1/Loyal North Lancashires ate their emergency rations without permission on 29 August 1914 and their lieutenant threw their rum away. The next day someone pinned up a little poem on the RSM's door:

> This place marks the spot
> Where many a young soldier lost his lot.
> It was poured out in damn dirty fashion
> Because he had eaten his emergency ration.

Grey Hens

The famous rum jar (also the name given to a heavy German mortar bomb) was a heavy, grey and brown earthenware vessel, popularly known as a 'grey hen'. Normally they held two gallons (if the recipients were in luck) although one-gallon containers were in use by 1916. The smaller one-gallon jars were later converted to stoneware bottles, sent up several at a time in openwork wooden cases. When the 2/West Yorkshires relieved a Devon battalion in December 1916 the latter's CSM left one of these bottles for the incoming troops, a typical example of the sharing mentality of the typical Tommy. In a trench occupied by the 7/Royal Warwickshires early in 1917 a fragment of 'sausage' bomb struck one of these rum cases, but only one bottle was broken. So the soldiers were surrounded by a gorgeous aroma whilst still having some rum to drink.

'Char-wallahs'

Men were not forced to drink rum. They had a right to refuse it and some did and were known as 'char-wallahs' or 'wad-shifters'. They had various reasons for refusal. Frank Dunham and his chums were stretcher-bearers. They thought that the 'beaucoup Tom Thumb' being dished out with the cocoa at 3am on 7 June 1917 (Battle of Messines) would hamper their work the next day. This point of view was shared by Dick Richards, an old soldier of the 2/RWF. He thought it made soldiers reckless. Private Pearson steadfastly turned down rum because of memories of his father (and others in Hull) spending their wages on drink while their wives and children went hungry.

Some men only wished to appear teetotal. As the 9/Royal Irish Rifles prepared to go over the bags on the first day of the Battle of the Somme (the 'Black Day' of the British Army) on 1 July 1916, a soldier whispered to his CO, Frank Crozier, 'Goodbye, sir! Good luck! Tell 'em I died a teetotaller. Just put it on a stone – if you can find me!' He was the biggest boozer in the battalion.

Four

Fags

'Gaspers'

Tommy relied more continuously on cigarettes than tea or rum because he could light up at any time – so long as he had a fag (or fag end) and a match to light it. It was a craving like those for tea and rum: he couldn't get enough of them. Cigarettes were a relief and solace for frayed nerves: you could puff away whilst awaiting the next bullet or shell. To be short of cigarettes was agony. George Coppard once tried dry tea leaves rolled in some brown paper because he was out of fags: it was horrible.

Second Lieutenant Norman Collins of the 1/6/Seaforth Highlanders, although agreeing that smoking was a great comfort, reckoned that most of the ration cigarettes were hardly worth smoking. He never inhaled from them. But men would re-light any sort of fag, even when it was almost down to nothing and saturated in tar and nicotine. It was not only for the nerves but also to ward off pangs of hunger. Like tea, rum and cocoa and cooking breakfast, having a smoke was an occasion for camaraderie with your pals. In unison they puffed and dragged away, indulging in cheerful obscenity.

Ration Fags

The official ration varied, depending on what was available, what the weather was like and the intensity of the warfare. The issue was irregular, to say the least. Major-General Whincop, whom we met in the

Supper in a billet at Berles-au-Bois, September 1915. Drawing by Les Read.

previous chapter as a 'no-rum' commander, was also opposed to the issue of cigarettes. It was his considered view that smoking impaired military efficiency just as much as rum (he also disliked steel helmets, which, in his view, made men soft).

The ration issues tended to get better later in the war, although Sergeant Beechey of 2/Lincolnshires recalled that they got 'plenty' in the Loos trenches in September 1915. But Private Braid only received sixteen cigarettes on Sunday night (3 August 1915) for the whole week to come. The general memory was of an issue of the order of twenty to thirty a week behind the lines but more in the front line. The issue during major battles could be generous. On the Somme the London Rifle Brigade received six tins of fifty for six days, showing that Tommy could smoke fifty a day if the cigarettes were available.

The 11/Royal Fusiliers, waiting to go over on the first morning of the Somme, were each given a packet of ten Woodbines, and Lieutenant Richard Hawkings was smoking an Abdullah as he led the attack. Smiler Marshall, according to his own account, had an issue of fifty Gold Flake and fifty Players, both well-regarded brands, plus two packs of ten Players every fortnight in 1918, plus a box of matches – crucial and sometimes in short supply.

Boosting the Ration

The ration issue was not enough for most Tommies so they had to acquire cigarettes by other means. Private Edge of B Company, 2/RWF, known to all and sundry as 'Sunny Jim', had a job in a canteen. On 21 August 1916 he walked seven miles to the trenches occupied by the Fusiliers because he thought they might like some extra 'cigawettes', as he pronounced them. He sold out in no time at all and walked the seven miles back.

Tommies could also get loved ones to send them cigarettes. Writing home on 12 September 1915 Lieutenant Spicer of the 9/King's Own Yorkshire Light Infantry asked for twenty Gold Flake and twenty-five Turkish or Egyptian brands.

Another good source, grim as it sounds, was dead soldiers' pockets and packs. Albert Bullock and a pal found 200 Woodbines on a corpse at Passchendaele. A 'fag', incidentally, meant a Woodbine to Tommy.

Special gifts of cigarettes, particularly at Christmas time, were a welcome boost to normal supply. A forage cart called on the 2nd Field Company, Royal Engineers on 7 August 1915 with a gift of 250 Woodbines for each sapper.

Short of Fags

There were many times when Tommy was short of fags, even if he had enough cash to buy them. There were severe shortages in 1914 – not only of cigarettes but tobacco and matches as well, at a time when the supply system was evolving and trying to cope with the rapid movement to and fro of the front line, at least until November.

The 17/Leicesters even ran out of the precious fag ends which soldiers kept in little tins (suitable for two draws and a fit of coughing) after stand-down at the beginning of the Battle of Arras in April 1917.

Smoking was sometimes banned when offensives were about to commence. This was the case on the night of 19 November 1917 when the onslaught at Cambrai was imminent. It was going to be a surprise tank attack so extreme caution was being exercised in order not to give the enemy any clues about the gathering forces.

The shortage of cigarettes was considered even worse than the shortage of food. If Tommy, searching frantically in the deep recesses of his pockets, came across a stubby fag end (known as a 'nicky') then he cheered up immensely.

Woodbine Willie

The cyclists of the 25/London were without a smoke for several days in December 1917 until the padre arrived with two per man. In fact, padres were often around to hand out the odd fag or two to men obviously in need of something to relieve their stress or pain. The most famous of these was 'Woodbine Willie', always ready with a cigarette for a wounded man. He was the Reverend Geoffrey Anketell Studdart Kennedy. He also came into the trenches to chat to the men, share a cup of char, tell jokes and say prayers with them. He was a chain-smoker himself.

At the Battle of Messines in June 1917 he ran out into No Man's Land under murderous fire to tend to the wounded or dying – British and German. He carried a wooden cross. He was awarded the Military Cross. He died after the war, still a young man, and they placed Woodbines on his coffin.

Corporal Clifford (1/Hertfordshires) was wounded as he crossed the Steenbeck Stream in the Third Battle of Ypres in 1917. As he lay in the liquid mud a padre came by and dropped a tin of Woodbines by his side. Bullets flew around them.

Fags in Extremis

The wounded in aid posts searched desperately in their pockets for a fag end and a light, or reached out with trembling hands to take a trusty Woodbine from a mate or a medical orderly and sank back as they inhaled the first few delicious draws. Tommy asked for a fag when nearing death to smooth the path to oblivion. When Trooper Walter Becklade of the 5th Cavalry Brigade was carried to a casualty clearing station there was a chap next to him with both his arms swathed in bandages. Becklade managed to find the man's pipe and lit it for him. Sadly, he could find nowhere to place it because his lower jaw had been blown away. At least the poor devil could smell his favourite baccy.

Private S.T. Sherwood fell into a shell-hole and became stuck in the glue-like mud in the Ypres Salient in 1917 with a German corpse for company. As he sank further and further, hour on hour, he calmly smoked his pipe. He was eventually rescued. Lieutenant John Glubb also remembered 'Old' Sapper Beardmore with almost an arm blown off sedately puffing away. Soldiers on field punishments for misdemeanours had their cigarettes confiscated – even ones they had bought with their own money – and were not allowed to smoke for the duration of the punishment – sometimes twenty-eight days.

As matches were often in short supply there was a substitute of a lighter with a thick corded wick providing a smouldering glow. A light from a single match could only be used twice because of a powerful superstition that if a third man attempted to use it disaster was around the corner.

When a man was ill, say with trench fever, he also craved a fag or pipe. Billy Nevill had a rotten headache for five days in January 1916 after dining on some tinned prawns and tinned pheasant. He discovered that Savory and Moore's 'Camels' eased the pain considerably. It was the same with toothache, belly aches and boils. A fag took Tommy's mind off pain.

A smoke could also partially block out nasty tastes and smells such as poison gas, explosives, and rotting corpses. Lance-Corporal Henry Ogle (7/Royal Warwicks) smoked 'Digger Mixture' in a corn cob pipe to repel the stench of unwashed bodies.

Woodbines and the Rest

The favourite brand, in terms of quality considered against cost, was Woodbines. Thomas Wilbansen of the Royal Scots Fusiliers remembered that they gave him a sermon and two packets of Woodbines when he embarked for France for the first time. The tobacco in them was mature, something that could not be said about a lot of the brands dished out as rations. These generally contained green tobacco, giving off an acrid rather than a sweet taste. Alfred Burrage described the taste as akin to seaweed.

Once again, profiteers made a lot of money out of these 'gasper' swindles, their great sounding names – 'White Cloud', 'Ruby Queen', 'Red Hussar' – being the only thing that was good about them. Inside these packs were the cards of the donors but they had been ripped off by contractors.

From parcels, canteens and some French shops Tommy could get his Woodbines, the real 'fag', or, if the pay ran to it, more expensive Virginian or Turkish ('stinkers'). Many British officers smoked Turkish or Abdullah (Egyptian). Lieutenant Vaughan of the 1/8/Royal Warwickshires, on the Steenbeck bog in the Ypres Salient (27 August 1917), took out his prized box of Abdullah but at that second there was an enemy attack and the precious cigarettes went flying into the mud. Yet it turned out the Germans were not attacking – a group of them just wanted to surrender – and Vaughan was able to retrieve his precious Egyptians. Indeed, trying to keep smokes dry in these conditions was a perennial problem.

In price, Woodbines generally stood between gaspers and the better, more popular brands such as Gold Flake, Players and Three Castles.

Lieutenant Spicer of the 9/King's Own Yorkshire Light Infantry paid seven pence for a pack of ten Woodbines in a French shop on 20 April 1916. During this year you could get ten gaspers for five pence in the big Army canteens, but thirty centimes in battalion canteens – between three and four pence. John Brophy and Eric Partridge remembered them as ten for sixpence. Prices rose ten to fifteen per cent in 1917 as the German submarine threat began to bite. Tommy relied more and more on the rations and parcels.

Looking at the war overall, a packet of the cheaper cigarettes cost Tommy about half a day's pay, so they were not really cheap. The price of a packet could buy you a meal or several cheap drinks. But cigarettes were addictive: men who arrived on the Western Front as non-smokers found it very difficult not to succumb to the habit. Billy Nevill held out for six months. Frank Dunham of 25/London also gave in on 17 November 1916 when he was cold and miserable in Rouen.

Woodbines were often used as a type of currency, such as two for a haircut. There was trade between cigarettes and rum, according to taste. Contents of parcels could be swapped for Woodbines. Frank Dunham got back late from leave on 30 December 1917 but the gift of a tin of Gold Flake to Sergeant Sturt meant he wasn't reported.

Rolling Your Own

Many Tommies saved money by using ration tobacco and Rizla cigarette papers to roll their own. Even if they had to buy good, inexpensive tobacco like BVD they were still able to economise.

Bill Collins of the 38 Machine-Gun Company rolled his own using a pungent dark shag. He stored the results in his cap. The look of bliss on his face as he lit up the first one in the morning was vastly enjoyed by his chum, George Coppard. George had a couple of puffs on one and it made his head reel. French home-grown tobacco was spongy and black and gummed together with spit, and not many Tommies tried it out, and never twice.

Trooper George Jameson (1/Northumberland Hussars) found some Belgian tobacco hanging in a loft. He pulled down some veins of it, rolled them up with a piece of thread and attempted to smoke the resulting creation; it was horrible.

Gifts

Parcels were eagerly awaited for precious Woodbines, Gold Flake and Players. Tommies would share with pals who were short of cigarettes. This sort of generosity sometimes spread to officers and other ranks. In April 1917 Siegfried Sassoon sent his batman to buy twelve dozen packs of Woodbines in their pale-green cardboard boxes from a YMCA canteen as an emergency supply for his company.

Captain Cosmo Clark of the 13/Middlesex was on the Amiens–Berteaucourt road in April 1918 when Winston Churchill came past in one of a line of four staff cars. All the staff officers emptied their cigarette cases and handed their contents over to Clark for his men, and Churchill donated some cigars (perhaps Corona, a 'Zeppelin' of a cigar). When men of 2nd Lieutenant Edmonds's Company did not get their rum he shared around his spare pack of the highly desirable De Reszkes. They would have preferred Woodbines.

Generous gifts from home abounded. When George Coppard was returning from leave at Victoria Station on 26 January 1916 he was showered with cigarettes, chocolates and hot drinks.

A love of smoking sometimes brought enemies together. Many of the exchanges in the Christmas Truce of 1914 were of cigarettes and cigars. German prisoners were often desperate for a smoke, and Private Read (17/Leicesters) found some squashed Gold Flake to give to one. When a sergeant of the 2/Queen's shot a German in the attack on Fontaine (23 April 1917) and was shot in return he laid down his rifle and presented his adversary with some water and a fag. They staggered off together holding each other up, puffing away, to the dressing station. When George Coppard was shot through the thigh (30 November 1917) he shared his cigarettes out with prisoners deputed to carry him to the aid post as a bribe to do the job carefully.

Tobacco and Pipes

A lot of Tommies, especially officers, smoked pipes. As with cigarettes, there were bitter complaints about the quality of the ration tobacco. The rotten stuff, also like 'gaspers', had fancy names, unheard of before being invented by con merchants. But you could buy decent baccy in the canteens, with probably the make 'BDV' as the 'Woodbine' of tobacco. It was Private Herbert Boorer's favourite and the same can be said for many thousands of Tommies. Also popular were Carlyle, Chairman, Player's Navy Mixture and Three Nuns. Officers settling down after duty could count on this as a touch of normal life in a hell-hole. J.B. Priestley, an officer in the 10/Duke of Wellingtons at Loos in September 1915, had no hot food in the trench and was living on cold bully beef and hard biscuits. His only solace was to puff away on his pipe. There were less comfortable moments: Captain John Staniforth's main thought as he waited to go over the top on the first day of the Battle of the Somme was how he was going to keep his pipe alight.

Back in Arras for a week in August 1916 Guy Chapman's clearest memory was of sitting under the chestnut trees in Place de la Prèfecture reading and smoking his pipe. Before the Battle of the Somme commenced, in June 1916, an officer of the 11/Royal Fusiliers sent a request to Dunhill's for a nice pipe. They sent him twelve samples, each in its own nice little box. Dunhill's asked him to choose one for himself and perhaps see if fellow officers would like any of the others. The lieutenant fell in love with a beautiful French Briar and returned the rest of the pipes; it set him back fourteen shillings and sixpence, about two days' pay, but he thought it was worth it.

Five

Supplying the Front

The System

The supply system for food and drink which evolved over the war was generally successful in sustaining between one and two million men in the war zone for over four years. It thus played a part in the final victory. The BEF grew to nearly two million by the end of 1917 with 1,250,000 combatants, who were harder to feed than non-combatants. By this time 32,000 tons of meat and 44,000 tons of bread (twenty times as much as in 1914) were moved to the front every month.

A huge and elaborate infrastructure and transport system met these colossal and ever-increasing demands without a complete breakdown, even in the rapid retreats of 1914 (when the system was in its infancy) and 1918. There were existing advantages, not least the highly developed and complex network of railways and roads of two industrialised nations. There were also extensive and well-equipped ports at Le Havre, Rouen and Boulogne to complement Southampton, Folkestone and Dover for the transit of food and drink (and much else). The distances between these places were relatively short and so were the distances from the French ports to the front.

Also, a largely static front was a major advantage in terms of supply – the system could grow without having to rapidly and constantly stretch or contract. The only hitches occurred when it *was* required to do so – in 1914 over a relatively brief period of a few weeks and during the German advance in 1918, which slowed down dramatically after a slightly longer period.

Advance was much less difficult to manage than retreat because the war did not descend on supply routes but simply obliged them to extend. Advances in the major British offensives were only of the order of a few miles. The more extensive advance of 1918 was drawn out over about three months and was still over a relatively limited distance (it never reached Germany).

A fleet of fourteen ferry boats out of Southampton and twelve out of Dover and Folkestone evolved. These were formerly cross-Channel passenger packets of about 2,000 tons. Their interiors were stripped out to provide extra capacity. No bunks or galleys were needed because of the short journeys. Supplies were unloaded at the ports or base depots, and broken down into train wagon loads and sent by rail to regulating stations. Base depots had forty-five butcheries and forty-eight bakeries.

At regulating stations the goods were unloaded to be taken on to advanced supply depots designed for the work of making up divisional trains – a trainload for each division. These went up to the railheads, usually ten to fifteen miles from the front line. Here the supplies were transferred to motor lorries driven by Army Service Corps (ASC) personnel by road to divisional refilling points. In some cases, the railhead was the refilling point if the distance to the front was much less than ten miles.

At the refilling point, divisional or brigade supply officers took over, using their own transport and manpower. Goods were divided into dumps, one for each unit to be supplied. Quartermasters from each unit were stationed here to organise the onward journey of supplies. The usual mode of transport from the dumps to the transport lines near the communication trenches was by horse-drawn general service (GS) wagon. Depending on the distance involved, mules might be used.

By late 1916, there were more and more light railways (*Decauville*) along which trucks could be pushed to the communication trenches. The first job my father had near the front in 1917 was to help clear the way for a light railway to Achiet-le-Grand on the old Somme battlefield. Frank Dunham was at Lankhof Dump on 27 December 1916 with a party of men sent to push well-loaded trucks on the light railway running out of the dump. Four men propelled each truck. Dunham remembered being frequently under fire and hiding behind the truck. It took from 10am to 2.30pm to get the truck up to a communication trench.

Once supplies reached the communication trench everything was usually carried on by hand by ration parties, although there were a few experiments with pack ponies and carts pulled by big dogs. At Bois Grenier in April 1915 the 2/RWF employed one of these animals (of 'mixed ancestry') called Thomas.

The task of maintaining and building railways and roads was gigantic. By 1918 about 40,000 men were labouring on roads and 29,000 on railways, supervised by the Royal Engineers' Railway Operating System. In addition, there were 11,000 labourers in the docks and another 8,000 engaged in other transport and communications jobs. Many of these were Indians, Egyptians, Chinese and other foreign nationals.

Transport was slow with a 12mph speed limit on Army trains, each one capable of carrying half a battalion. The sheer volume of traffic tended to lower actual speeds to about 5mph, so, despite the limited distances, it could take days to move goods up to the front line. Frozen points and signals made the situation worse in bad weather.

A British Director of Railways worked in liaison with the French railway authorities from November 1914. In the autumn of 1916 Sir Eric Geddes was appointed as Inspector-General of Transportation to iron out growing problems. After detailed statistical analysis he divided the system into four distinct parts – docks, light railways (which rapidly developed under his leadership), railways and roads. In the year he was at the helm an already efficient system was transformed into a model of modern organisation.

The Army Service Corps (ASC)

The bulk of supervisory and operating personnel on the roads were in the ASC, which numbered 160,000 in 1918 (twenty-five times bigger than in 1914). Despite their invaluable work the infantry generally had a poor opinion of them, mostly, however, because the ASC's pay was six times as much as theirs and because they did not have to endure the perils and miseries of the trenches.

The infantry called the ASC 'Ally Sloper's Cavalry' (Ally Sloper was a character in a weekly comic). When the prefix 'Royal' was granted to the ASC in 1918 it then became known as 'Run Away, Someone's Coming'.

When refilling points were near the support areas, however, ASC drivers could come under fire. Corporal Henry Gregory (119 Machine-Gun Company) remembered drivers flinging themselves to the ground when this happened. He advised them to keep upright and still because bullets at this particular spot tended to come in low and it was better to get hit in the leg rather than the head.

Enemy Attacks on Supply Routes

Increasingly, slow-moving and crowded supply lines came under attack. Lieutenant-Colonel N. Fraser-Tytler of D/151 Battery, Royal Garrison Artillery, described the road between Maricourt and Suzanne as crammed with convoys of up to 300 GS wagons. This seven-mile journey usually took six hours.

Captain Dunn, the MO of the 2/RWF, wrote in August 1915 that both sides tended not to aim at rations transport near the front line. But by the latter months of the Battle of the Somme in the winter of 1916 it was standard artillery practice on both sides to target rations coming up to the front, frequently causing loss and delay.

By this time, too, German heavy bombers routinely bombed and machine-gunned the ration dumps, depots and railheads. Both Alfred McLelland Burrage and my father remembered arriving in Poperinghe late in 1917 to be greeted by air attacks on the railway sidings.

Coping with Advance

Although it was the rapid retreats of 1914 and 1918 which caused the worst food supply problems (see Chapter Thirteen), rapid advance did stretch transport routes. The move from the River Marne in September 1914 took front-line units forty miles from the railheads. The advance of 1918 was held up to some extent because railways could not keep up with the front. There were experiments with drops from aircraft. This had been tried first in January 1917 when supplies were dropped to troops surrounded by water near Houthulst. Following the Battle of Messines in June 1917 – a remarkable all-round success – new roads were quickly built up to the old front line.

Back-room Boys

Quartermasters and transport officers and COs performed valiantly, with long hours of unremitting toil, to try to ensure that men got their food at the correct time and place. On 5 September 1918 the fast-moving front at Moslains and the Canal du Nord meant that the 1/19/Londons could not make up ration parties and the QM and other HQ staff carried the rations up to the front line themselves, typical of the efforts of 'back-room boys' to see that Tommy did not go hungry or thirsty. Similarly, 2nd Lieutenant Cyril Rawlings, a battalion transport officer, rode about on horseback with little rest for five days from 29 September to 4 October 1915 at Loos to get ration limbers – small carts – through to the right places in the heat of battle.

Captain Jack, a company commander with the 1/Cameronians at Buzancy, also directed ammunition and ration wagons and carts for twenty hours on 13 September 1914. He did the same sort of thing during the First Battle of Ypres on 21 October. When things became quieter at night in the trenches Tommy could hear the rumbling wheels of the British ration limbers and also the Germans' carts.

Hot Food on the Spot

As the static trench lines settled down early in 1915 there were increasing demands for hot food to be sent up to the Tommies. Commanders realised the advantages of this to morale and health and thus military efficiency. Mobile company field kitchens ('cookers') were gradually established near the transport lines, where cooks could pick up rations and prepare stew or soup and tea or cocoa.

When the static warfare persisted some cooks were even sent further forward to front-line trenches, very often on a shift basis where cooks took turns to be in the trenches. The advantage this brought was hot food on the spot; the disadvantage was that the cooks only had limited cooking equipment and they suffered like Tommy from enemy action and the weather. They had special dugouts, but even so they often worked under appalling and frightening conditions. Going to and fro along the communication trenches was also arduous and dangerous.

Eternal rum problems. Cartoon by Bruce Bairnsfather.

However, this arrangement was generally only put into practise during quiet periods on the front. At times of prolonged bombardment and preparation for attack or defence the cooks stayed back. On other particular nights, cooks coming up from the transport lines might fail to arrive or be very late because they suffered the same difficulties faced by ration parties.

Hazardous Journeys for Ration Parties

Ration parties were usually selected nightly from each company to go and collect supplies. However, there were some semi-permanent groups specialising in this task stationed in the transport lines.

Being selected to go back for the rations was generally dreaded. Sometimes men cut cards for the duty – with ace low – but a rota system was the fairest way. It meant a double journey taking hours as the communication trench was usually around half a mile long, often longer – at Ribecourt the 1/19/Londons had to go back nearly a mile in January 1918. Going back to the transport lines could be easier because there was less weight to carry – empty containers mostly. However, even this journey could be made hazardous by enemy action and the weather, both of which could render the communication trench very treacherous.

The trek was in the dark along slippery, wobbly or broken duckboards and through areas where the trench had been badly damaged, so that men sometimes fell into deep holes. The containers – dixies or hay boxes – were carried by two or more men and if one lost his footing the others could go down with him. The handles on dixies were made of thin white metal and dug into the carriers' hands.

The language got worse and worse. There was corner after corner to negotiate (the trench was zig-zagged to diminish the effects of shell blasts and to make sitings by enemy machine-gunners or snipers more difficult) with people on other tasks, such as messengers or the walking wounded or those on stretchers, coming the other way. Stretcher-bearers had their own communication trench but when casualties were very high they were forced to use the normal trench as well. When this occurred the ration party had to climb out of the trench and could be lit up by enemy flares, with potentially disastrous results.

Coming back could be a lot worse than going because of the bulk and weight of what they had to convey. Show a light or make too much noise and you could attract enemy fire. Tacit 'arrangements' not to fire on each others' ration parties went by the board in the later stages of the Battle of the Somme. They became fair game for the enemy artillery.

The double journey took hours, sometimes all night; on 8 July 1917 Frank Dunham was part of a ration crew whose journey took five and a half hours. Men returned covered in mud, cuts and bruises, totally exhausted. There were diversions, too: machine-gun posts, forward observers, signallers or men digging trenches forward into No Man's Land ('saps') had to be fed.

Up Top

Often ration parties had to cross open land, with sometimes very unclear routes. Trenches could be impassable because of damage or floods. The party from the 1/5/Royal Warwickshires at Gommecourt Wood in January 1916 scrambled across half a mile of muddy fields to six muddy front-line trenches in freezing cold weather. Luckily for them, this was at a time when the enemy was less likely to fire on a ration party.

On 12 December 1914, in the Ypres Salient, the 1/Cameronians found the communication trench completely blocked and had to take the rations and other stores (sometimes these men could be lumbered with other stores, such as coal, coke or charcoal, or even great bundles of barbed wire, making progress in the trench even more hazardous) across open land. As did the 17/Leicesters a year later at Berles-au-Bois.

About the same time, George Coppard (2/Queen's Royal West Surreys – 6 December 1915) also had to stumble across open fields with his chums near Givenchy. But he was in luck because he discovered a soup kitchen up there. On the next night volunteers for ration party duty flocked forward.

On the other hand, up top could be easier because of hollows or dips in the terrain. Ration parties were forced up top on the battle-fields of the Third Battle of Ypres because of flooded land which was pockmarked with millions of almost continuous shell holes and lacking in proper deep trenches. All that the party from the 2/Devons found in October 1917 was a series of water-filled holes with a few sandbags stacked on their forward rims.

What each man had to carry varied from night to night. He could be encumbered with a heavy, stew-filled dixie which he might carry with his mate on a pole. 'Hay boxes' were used later in the war. These were oblong containers which were insulated. A special frame was designed for these, carried by four men. But it could be a couple of petrol cans of water or tea, the handles of which also cut into your hand. You could sling the cans together over your shoulder but they bumped all the way. You could have rum jars or cigarette tins, or butter tins. It could be sandbags of bacon or cheese, or tea and sugar (mixed already – hard luck if you happened to be one of those odd Tommies who liked tea without sugar!).

Disasters

Misfortune could easily befall ration parties, perhaps resulting in their complete non-arrival. All the men in one from the 2/West Yorkshires were killed on 10 November 1916 on the Somme. A detail carrying officers' food (composed of their batmen or servants) was wiped out in Polygon Wood in September 1914. Another ration party, coming along behind, picked up the sandbags and the company was treated to cooked sausages in tins and several loaves of bread, at a time when fresh bread was scarce (and Tommy never had many sausages).

On 6 October 1917 Lieutenant Edmonds (5/Royal Warwickshires) went back looking for his ration party which was supposed to be coming up to the Stroombeck stream area (the shell hole-strewn Passchendaele battlefield) and found them in a deep alcoholic sleep induced by consuming all the rum (and food) for the company. On recovery they said they had got lost. Edmonds was not impressed. Ration parties, of course, could genuinely get lost in the maze of trenches in the dark. The one from the 12/East Surreys became lost on 31 December 1917. What a way to bring in the New Year. They arrived at their company's position on 2 January 1918.

Individuals in the party could become separated. If you lost touch with the man in front of you it could spell trouble. The idea was to follow the lead NCO, who was supposed to know the way and the hazards. At times when it became apparent to him that his party was in disarray he had to turn back to sort it out. This happened between the Hooge crater and Glencourse Wood in the Ypres Salient on 15 September 1917. It took till dawn for the corporal to get his men together and deliver the rations.

The State of the Grub

Even if it did arrive in one piece, accidents could well reduce the quantity and quality of the food and drink. A Tommy of the 1/8/Worcesters in the Ancre Valley late in 1915 trod on a loose duckboard and dropped a dixie full of stew into some icy water. All he managed to retrieve were a few carrots floating in gravy. In the same party Private H. Raymond Smith met a kitchen orderly to pick up some sacks of dry rations and a rum jar. Unfortunately, he forgot to pick up the jar. When he went back to get it in the pitch black night he accidentally kicked it over; luckily for him and his company the stopper stayed on.

It was extremely difficult to keep dry rations dry. Tea and sugar often suffered because of this. Lieutenant W.S. Dane of the Seaforth Highlanders, who did prefer unsweetened tea, blamed the 'Brass Hats' (HQ staff) for the fact that tea and sugar was mixed (and the weather). You had to blame someone. The men who thought the tea wasn't sweet enough blamed the Brass Hats as well.

Another commodity which suffered in sandbags was bread. It could arrive in a sorry, soggy state and covered in mud. There was nothing worse than a morass of bread mixed with fibres from the bags, although Frank Dunham discovered a bullet in one such quagmire on 27 December 1916 and wondered whether soggy bread had saved someone's life.

Bacon for breakfast was also vulnerable. Damp and mud could be wiped off successfully: the grit was more of a problem. However, throughout it all, Tommy mostly retained his sense of humour. One party of the 7/Royal Warwickshires arrived in the trenches at Hébuterne on 10 August 1915 stark naked except for boots and helmets, dixies slung on their shoulders. Those awaiting their grub gave them a rousing and ribald welcome.

Six

Cookers

'Tommy Cookers'

Some battalions had to wait a long time before their cooks came anywhere near them: it didn't happen for the 2/RWF until September 1915. Until then it was cold meat or bully beef and biscuits, bread if the Fusiliers were lucky, jam and butter and some tinned fruit on a good day. If they wanted some hash or stew and some tea they had to cook it themselves. Some types of 'Tommy Cooker' were basically a chunk of solidified fuel on a stand. Bryant and May's 'Kampite' came in a container resembling a large box of matches: there were six fuel blocks with wicks, and a stand. When not in use Tommy could just stick it in a pocket. More elaborate products, such as the tri-winged, foldable job, were still designed to be small and portable. The other big advantage of the Tommy Cooker was that it was smokeless. Smoke was a giveaway for snipers.

The Cooker could be lit under a D-shaped canteen or mess tin acting as a cooking pot. It was a metal plate with sides all round, a lid (which like the much bigger lid of the dixie could be used as a frying pan) and a handle. Soldiers also had a mug for hot liquid, usually tea, and a knife, fork and tablespoon, although they used the spoon on its own a lot (which said a lot for the sort of food they were eating).

Alfred Burrage calculated that it took two hours to boil half a pint of water but other estimates suggest one and a half pints in two hours. Len Beechey of the 18/London Irish (in a letter home on 5 April 1917) reckoned he could boil one and a half pints 'in not too long a time'. To heat tins it also took hours.

Tommy Cookers could be purchased in Army canteens or from stores back home. Captain Billy Nevill was sent a grander affair fuelled by solid paraffin wax, bought from the Army and Navy Stores in London. He could make excellent cocoa with it. Some divisions provided Tommy Cookers and a fresh slab of fuel per man every day.

Primus Stoves

Hotter than the Tommy Cooker was the primus stove, fuelled by methylated spirits or paraffin. Even the 'baby' primus, which you could also carry in your pocket, was more expensive than the Tommy Cooker, however, and usually beyond the pocket of individual Tommies. But a group of pals could invest in one, as Frank Hawkings and his mates did in August 1915. They heated water and tins far quicker than Tommy Cookers. Private Kenneth Gary of the Honourable Royal Artillery had his own baby primus with a spare tin of spirit and also a Tommy Cooker with a spare refill. He wasn't taking any chances.

Many officers had their own primus ('baby' ones or larger). Sydney Rogerson had one of the larger variety, along with a 'scoff box' – containing plates, cups and coffee pots. In 'Bivvy tins' the spirit lit up a lamp to provide heat and light.

The Mobile Kitchen

Company field kitchens or cookers were usually based on a design by the manufacturers Rusking and Hornby Ltd. They were mobile and followed the battalion around, to and from the front. The field kitchen was in two parts – a front limber which could be drawn by a horse or mules, and a back cooker attached to the front section. The front limber had two large wheels straddling four asbestos-lined compartments in which food was stored. Two large frying pans were strapped to the sides and two lockers contained cooking utensils, washing equipment and tools. Limbers were used for general carrying purposes, with boxed compartments or without, when they simply became a moving platform for boxes and drums.

The cooker section of the mobile kitchen had five eight-gallon steel containers for boiling food. Each container had a stove underneath it. There was a separate water boiler and two fuel containers holding coal or wood. The dixies – the word coming from the Hindustani 'degschai' – and the later 'hay boxes' were the portable containers to take away the food.

Keeping the Food Hot

The containers could be left on the cooker to be warmed up until taken off by the ration party or served directly to troops in the support areas. You could try to keep the stew or tea warm by putting the container in a sandbag and surrounding it with straw or hay. The real 'hay box' was based on the thermos flask principle of two skins. These could either be strapped to men's backs or carried by four men using frames.

An experiment in sending up soup in thermos flasks to the 2/RWF on the cold nights of January 1916 was not popular with long-serving soldiers, who preferred to make up their own stews with the remnants of their rations rather than submit to the uncertainties of someone else's concoctions. They also feared that the hot flasks would replace rum. The experiments were not repeated.

Another new-fangled idea was to wrap petrol cans in kapok and feathers. Perhaps the most sophisticated device of all was the 'Auto Bouillant', a self-heating tin of meat and vegetables. General Fanshaw (well known as 'The Chocolate Soldier' through his habit of presenting chocolate to subalterns whom he thought had done well) gave one to Lieutenant Vaughan of the 1/8/Royal Warwickshires near the Steenbeck stream on 27 August 1917.

Grander Cookers

The CO of the 7th Field Company of the Royal Engineers had a huge iron range which had to be dragged around by mules to the various campaigns. Lieutenant John Glubb tried to get rid of it on several occasions but the Major always managed to retrieve it.

A common way of acquiring superior equipment was to take it without leave, or from the enemy. On their advance from the Marne on 11 September 1914 the 2/RWF came across an abandoned mess cart near

Marisy St Geneviève. It was a glorious affair which the battalion used for the next three years. It was like a travelling shop – a light, four-wheeled cart with food trays inside and shutters on each side which could be let down to make counters. Similarly, the 1/Hull Pals captured a magnificent German field kitchen (along with the cooks) on 29 October 1918. It had a gleaming copper boiler. The Hull cooks were immensely proud of it, so much so that they took it back to Hull after the war. 377 Battery, Royal Artillery, also obtained a complete German cookhouse in a section of the Hindenburg Line on 20 November 1917 during the first day of the Battle of Cambrai, along with plenty of sausage and wine. The artillery ate very well that night.

Three sergeants from a Scottish battalion captured an enemy position during the Battle of Loos in September 1915. In a cellar they found an elderly officers' cook in a white coat (elderly on the Western Front meant about forty). A table was spread with a splendid meal and the sergeants ordered the cook to eat a bit of it to show that it wasn't poisoned. They then took over and ate the lot.

DIY Stoves

Even with relatively hot food coming from the cooks, Tommy was still keen to extend his heated diet; a great variety of stoves and braziers developed as a result. Some stoves were very basic – the 7/Royal Warwickshires made theirs from discarded biscuit tins and oil drums in the autumn of 1915. These were placed on platforms built up with clay. A tin pipe lagged with clay and with a cowel made from a jam tin carried away the fumes.

Sapper Arthur Sambrook's stove on the Loos front in 1916 was made from a large paint drum. It had a pipe (made of a flattened biscuit tin hammered round a pole) leading from the dugout. Sambrook decided to play a prank on his mates huddled for warmth round the stove. He dropped a piece of 'mature' camembert down the pipe and blocked off the top of it. Gas helmets were donned below.

Good quality stoves were highly prized and needed protection from other Tommies on the prowl. When the 2/West Yorkshires moved into the Somme front in November 1916 the CO, Lieutenant Colonel Jack, called on each company commander, including Sidney Rogerson of

B Company. Jack congratulated Rogerson for having such an enterprising servant. They had only been in the trenches for a few hours yet Rogerson's man had already stolen the colonel's stove whilst his batman wasn't looking.

Braziers

Braziers were popular but were generally the smokiest of Tommy's cookers and were the first to be banned for that reason. Tommy had ways of circumventing this restriction, including deafness. A lot of braziers were simply drums or tins with holes drilled in their sides. But lucky units were issued with manufactured braziers complete with a ration of charcoal to fuel them.

The other problem with braziers was the fumes emanating from them in dugouts or even funk holes, and cellars in billets. Coke braziers were banned by the CO of the 8/East Surreys in late 1915 but they simply sprouted chimneys. The MO of the 2/RWF, Captain James Dunn, found Sergeant Jones in a fume-filled cellar blue-faced and stertorous alongside Dunn's servant, another Jones, who was, apparently, deceased. They wrapped him in a blanket in the open, a fresh wind blew up from the east, and Jones came to life and went to sleep.

Fuel

Finding fuel for stoves, braziers or open fires was a perennial problem. Coal was always scarce, especially in cold weather, a time of scorched knees and frozen backs. Because coke had dangerous fumes the less toxic charcoal was sometimes issued. The cyclists of the 25/London searched through a ditched tank on 9 December 1915 and came across a can of petrol. Burnt underground, however, this discharged toxic black smoke and blackened their faces.

In light of shortages, there was often a need to rely on wood. Ration and ammunition boxes soon disappeared. Nothing wooden was safe – the A-shaped trench frames, cross pieces of duckboards, the duckboards themselves, and hurdling boards all went as the weather got colder. The loss of these trench supports made the effects of poor weather even worse. Sadly, even crosses from graves vanished. Replacements took time to arrive because of a general shortage of wood (whole woods were being cut down to bolster supplies) and the reluctance of QMs to make good the depredations – perhaps reasoning that if Tommy got wetter and muddier he would stop pinching the trench supports.

'Buggy'

Some Tommies were absolute experts in creating little fires out of almost nothing, happy to chip away at the wooden supports of the trench with bayonets or jack-knives. As early as December 1914 the 1/Cameronians in the Ypres trenches lit fires like this when coke for the braziers ran out. Corporal Robinson (otherwise known as 'Buggy'), a New Zealander in the 2/RWF, was the master of the improvised fire. He would make a small hole in the side of the trench and cover it with a piece of groundsheet pegged into the earth with rifle cartridges. His 'stove' was then positioned in this hole: it was a tin containing a piece of rifle-cleaning rag soaked in whale oil. From this he cajoled a very weak heat, yet enough to warm a mug of tea or cocoa without showing any light. When all other heaters were banned Buggy still had his hot drink. He also made omelettes by breaking eggs into his water bottle and shaking them around, just like a cocktail shaker.

Frank Hawkings, in Wulverghem in January 1915, used a tin of Vaseline and rifle rag to prepare some Oxo. J.B. MacLean made tea over a candle. Others made paper spills to boil water in mess-tins. If you were desperate for a cuppa the love letters had to go.

Cooks

There were many types of cooks. Stuart Dolden of the London Scottish had been a solicitor before the war but in 1916 he was a cook. Many cooks were older – in their thirties or forties or even older. Sergeant-cooks supervised company cooks. When the 2/RWF did not have one for a year the standard of food for the various companies differed significantly. When one appeared in October 1916 the food generally improved.

Many cooks were ex-butchers, selected because of their prowess with meat. In the event, they cooked an awful lot of bully beef rather than fresh or frozen meat. The nose cap of a small shell landed at a cook's feet on 4 January 1916 at Saulty. He stared at it disdainfully and remarked, 'What a pity it didn't hit the beef. I need something to make an impression on it.'

Cooks did come under enemy fire, even in the vicinity of the transport lines and certainly in the communication trenches. The field kitchen of the Connaught Rangers was hit by a shell on 21 March 1918 (the opening day of the big German offensive). A cook was sent flying but he picked himself up and carried on cooking breakfast.

Cooks were not renowned for cleanliness. Cookers were soon black and greasy, and so were the cooks as they stoked their fires and stirred their brews – usually with a smile and a joke. One officer complained to a cook about the litter of empty tins scattered about his field kitchen. 'Well, sir,' he replied, 'seeing as how they are building an insinuator I'll put 'em all in that, sir.' In contrast the cooks of the Connaught Rangers at Coulonby on 20 May 1917 cleaned everything spick and span – cookers, water carts, even the harnesses and the chains for the horses.

The skills of cooks varied greatly, hence the need for supervision. By late 1918, Frank Dunham (who had been a stretcher-bearer) graduated to the level of medical orderly. His MO had a brilliant cook (he was also the doctor's servant). On 2 November 1918, just north of Tournai, he produced a rabbit and vegetable stew of exceptional quality, plus superb sausages. 'Beaucoup manger' wrote Dunham in his diary.

An officer brought back some grouse from the Yorkshire Moors after a spot of leave, but due to transport delays they were crawling with maggots when he got back to his billet. Undeterred, his cook served up the bird with a nice white sauce for the officer and his companions. They were full of praise for the meal but little did they know that the sauce was made from the maggots. When Lieutenant Carr of 377 Battery, Royal Artillery, procured a chicken in Arras in November 1917 his cook burnt it to a cinder. To drown his sorrows, Carr drank a whole bottle of whisky and fell into a deep sleep. Lieutenant Blacker (4/Coldstream Guards) had a clean and willing cook but, according to Blacker, he was 'unversed in the culinary arts'.

Cooks in the trenches could find themselves suddenly with a lot of new friends, largely because their cookhouse dugouts were warm and cosy. It was a real treat for the 1/Londons to get Christmas dinner in the trench: producing a meal of quality in a hole in the ground in atrocious weather was a triumph. Private Jack Sweeney, a cook for the 1/Lincolns, remembered cooking with only an old pail over a coke fire; the officers he was cooking for insisted on a five-course meal. He still managed to brew some tea for the men at the same time and made sure they got anything the officers left. The Tommies drew as close as they could to the fire and the steam rose off their sodden clothes.

Meeting up with the company cooks as a battalion came out of the line was something that Tommy looked forward to. On 23 May 1918 the 2/RWF found the cookers brimming with piping hot 'burgoo' (porridge), which they considered to be scrumptious. The cyclists of the 25/Londons met their cooks at Havrincourt on 11 December 1917 and the cocoa and rum was memorable.

Supplying rations in the rest areas was not normally a problem. The balance between fresh or frozen meat and preserved meat was better. There were canteens, *estaminets* and parcels from home. But if something was not right the cooks could expect comment from the troops. On 2 August 1915 the 2nd Field Company, Royal Engineers, had a supper of soup, cheese and gingerbread, but the toast wasn't up to much. The cooks were informed of this quite plainly. The sappers were already in a bad mood because they were working hard in a 'rest' area chopping down Warnimont Wood near Hébuterne. Indeed, the infantry was also sometimes called upon to work when supposedly at rest when labour companies were not available. They were not happy about this and expected their grub to be better than usual.

If billets were some distance from the field kitchen, ration parties had to be provided and there was the usual problem of keeping the food hot. Sergeant Read of the 17/Leicesters in Lillers was half a mile away from the cookers (January 1917) so he organised the wrapping of the dixies in blankets.

Seven

Rations

The Ration Schedule

The official rations schedule of 1914 was intended to take into account the hard physical toil warfare entailed. The experts considered that 3,000 to 3,500 calories a day was reasonable in normal circumstances but decided that a figure of 4,193 calories would cover the additional work and also the effects of bad weather. In fact, the full proposed schedule of food added up to 4,279 calories when fresh or frozen meat and bread were supplied, or 4,625 if preserved meat and hard biscuits were used.

The staple diet of fresh or frozen meat (eighteen ounces – 1,112 calories) and bread (eighteen ounces – 1,184 calories), made up 2,296 calories and fifty-four per cent of the total schedule. The official substitutes of preserved meat and hard biscuits made up fifty-seven per cent of the total. Preserved meat provided 989 calories a day (sixteen ounces) but the biscuits, even at a ration of only twelve ounces, contained 1,653 calories, 469 more than eighteen ounces of bread.

The much-maligned 'dog' biscuit was therefore the biggest sustainer of all in terms of carbohydrates. No wonder they made a good fire. 'Old Bill', the main character of the Bruce Bairnsfather cartoons, certainly made use of them as he tried to get a fire going. The pangs of hunger were most likely to be subdued by the solid if unpopular Huntley and Palmer Mark 4 biscuit, or Mark 5 by 1917.

Fresh and Frozen Meat

Given that the actual ration in the trenches was more likely to be preserved meat and biscuits rather than fresh fare (because of supply difficulties), Tommy generally got more than the official daily total of calories. The ubiquitous stew meant that meat in any form was mostly going to be boiled with vegetables. A nice beef or lamb stew created variety and taste but Tommy's main concerns was that it should be hot and well-cooked, whatever was in it – and cooks produced many excellent bully beef or M and V stews.

Using fresh or frozen meat in stews was the easiest way to cook it and also the easiest way to get it up to the trenches. It had to be cooked quickly or the MO would come sniffing around and either condemn it or wash it in permanganate of potash, which didn't do the taste any good.

Bacon

Tommy was usually a happy man when his rashers were frying at dawn. Breakfast with bacon was special (see Chapter Eight). He could augment the ration by buying some bacon in the canteens in the rest areas but that would only last a day or two and he was likely to be in the support and front trenches for about a fortnight.

Bacon fat was almost as desirable. Wipe your bread in it and that was very tasty – to Tommy, at any rate. If the cooks were up there with them, eager queues for the fat formed round the dixie lids being used as frying pans.

The daily ration of bacon was supposed to be four ounces (349 calories), perhaps two or three rashers. It is well-nigh impossible with any of these ration items to say whether Tommy did get his due. There were one and a quarter million Tommies by the end of 1917, meaning just as many 'perambulating stomachs' and a wide spectrum of individual food and drink histories. In their reports, diaries and letters some Tommies seemed quite satisfied with what they got, others complained about some of it and others complained about all of it.

"Someone's been at this blinkin Strawberry"

Eternal jam problems. Cartoon by Bruce Bairnsfather.

Cheese

The cheese ration was three ounces a day (352 calories). There was usually some cheese knocking about somewhere in the trench to go with a slice of bread or a biscuit. Reading the diaries it seemed that there was more likely to be cheese than bread. Cheese (or some cheese) had the great advantage of probably tasting better the older it got even if you needed to put on your gas helmet to eat it.

Bread and Jam

In the diaries there are lots of complaints about the lack of bread. Because of this the amount received tended to be recorded and so it is possible to check this against the official daily ration (Chapter Eight). Hard biscuits were almost always available so the supply of carbohydrates was good. But, of course, you can't beat the taste of fresh bread.

Bread and jam was also a great favourite (the jam ration was four ounces – 296 calories). Tommy's main grouse here was that it was nearly always plum and apple jam – more monotony. It was another reason why the infantry hated the Army Service Corps which could usually boast about strawberry jam. Jam was more difficult to bring from the rest areas because it was in tins and Tommy was already carrying a heavy load up to the front. Later in the war it was in cardboard cartons (possibly by popular request).

Tommy could buy more ration items in a canteen or civilian outlet, but with pay of between one shilling and two shillings a day he was severely restricted in what he could buy, especially when you consider he also wanted cigarettes, egg and chips, wine, beer and coffee.

Private Braid (on 3 August 1915) and many others complained that currants, raisins and dates were being substituted for jam. Braid was not pleased because he had a suspicion that this was the dried fruit sent out by generous donors and the British Army was taking advantage of this to cut down the jam ration.

Rest of the Schedule

The schedule included eight ounces of fresh vegetables a day. The cooks usually managed this by adding potatoes, peas and carrots to the stew. The vegetables in the M and V tins were also part of the ration. There was a dried vegetable ration of two ounces – small, multi-coloured lumps which swelled up when soaked.

The tea ration was designed to enable Tommy to make six pints a day, nowhere near what he wanted, so he needed to stock up from the canteens (or rely on parcels or his pals). Whatever happened he was never going to drink weak tea.

The sugar ration was three ounces a day (335 calories) so Tommy would also need to augment this if three or four or more teaspoonfuls were going into his tea. The big ration of condensed milk (twelve ounces – 425 calories) helped enormously with sweetness in the tea. This was a larger volume of calories than in any other item in the schedule except meat, bread or biscuits. It also made up the sweetness lacking else-where in the diet apart from jam and sugar. This explained why Tommy got so hooked on tinned milk.

He was supposed to get one ounce of rice (thirty-four calories) and just below an ounce (102 calories) of oatmeal, usually in the form of porridge ('burgoo') which livened up breakfast considerably. However, it appeared that the rice ration was mainly saved up for the rest areas to make up decent quantities for meals. Alfred Burrage of the Artists' Rifles recalled that if there was porridge for breakfast there was no rice for dinner.

One item generally missing from the ration was eggs. How Tommy longed for an egg in the trenches. He was able to bring a few from the rest areas but, of course, they only lasted a short while. It was no surprise how much he looked forward to egg and chips in an *estaminet*.

Salt (0.5 ounce), pepper (.028 ounce) and mustard (.005 ounce) were in the schedule, popped into the stew, no doubt, and Tommy would have some more in his pocket to add, either into the stew or to liven up cold bully beef or M and V. Old soldiers had some curry powder.

Later Changes to the Schedule

Later in the war there were some changes to the ration schedule. Fresh or frozen meat was reduced to sixteen ounces from eighteen on 1 October 1915. Officially, this was achieved by supplying less bone in the meat. The ration of preserved meat was reduced from sixteen ounces to twelve, quite a drop, and significant since it was often substituted for fresh or frozen meat. There was also a reduction of mustard from .005 ounce to .002 on 22 October 1915, but an addition of one ounce of pickle a day was introduced in April 1916.

Condensed milk went up from twelve ounces a day to fifteen in April 1916, very good news for Tommy. But the news on jam was not so good – down from four ounces to three. However, a weekly butter ration of two ounces was introduced but this could be substituted by margarine ('axle grease') and usually was according to Winston Groom of the London Rifle Brigade. Sometimes four ounces a week appeared, but usually of margarine.

The preserved meat ration was restored to sixteen ounces in 1917 but fresh or frozen meat went down from sixteen ounces to twelve, an indication that the U–boat campaign was biting into supplies and that Tommy would get fewer beef and lamb stews. Bread was reduced from eighteen ounces to sixteen and biscuits from twelve ounces to ten. The ration of tea was halved, which meant that Tommy had to buy more of his own, placing an extra strain on his finances unless he got some in his parcels.

Sugar was also reduced by half an ounce; the official excuse was that there was plenty of sugar in the milk. Potatoes were becoming difficult to get and were substituted more and more by rice, oatmeal and currants. Dripping (meat fat) became a cash commodity for the Army, which sold it to buy other rations and extras.

By this time, the calorie count of the ration schedule which included fresh or frozen meat and bread was 3,655, which was around the figure for ordinary manual workers. The amount of work now required of the infantry in the trenches pointed to the need for a calorie total similar to that being suggested for the new US Army of 4,714 a day, about a third more than in the British schedule. Reliance on preserved meat and biscuits was clearer than ever, bringing in a daily calorie total of 4,349, still above the official daily target of 1914.

The rations for combatants generally exceeded that for non–combatants in every item of diet except vegetables and jam. This was in recognition of the availability of canteens and civilian establishments behind the lines and the fact that non–combatants were paid more.

Comparisons With Other Armies

Comparisons with the calorie content of the food given to the troops of other nations do not tell us much, except that the Americans did very well. The French were due 4,466 calories and there was many a Tommy tale of how tasty their meals were, certainly the impression of the 10/Duke of Wellingtons at Carency-Souchez in March 1916. They got about a pint of wine a day. On the other hand, there were plenty of reports of poor quality food.

German troops were supposed to receive 4,038 calories but evidence suggests they rarely got this much, especially by late 1917 when the Allied naval blockade of German coasts was beginning to take effect. Moreover, the quality of their food varied enormously, especially the bread: they were due twenty-four ounces a day but this was often made up of poor quality rye bread. The meat ration was only about five ounces and there was no sugar or milk.

Rationing in Britain

During 1917 Tommy's diet began to compare very favourably with what his folks back home were eating. When my father reached Mailly-Maillet in March 1917 his meals were better than he had been getting in London. By the summer of that year rationing was introduced in Britain and there were long queues at shops for food. Relatives tried to put on a brave face about it all when their soldier sons or husbands came home on leave, but it still worried soldiers to think that their loved ones were not eating properly. Major Rowland Fielding wrote to his wife on 21 October 1917 hoping that she was not having to queue for sugar and tea, commodities badly hit by the U-boat campaign, and that she was not half-starved. A lot of priority was given to getting tea and sugar to the front line because Tommy depended so much on his supplies of sweet tea.

By February 1918 the situation was even worse, with men taking joints of meat with them when they went on leave, and butter and sugar. When they got home they had to go to Food Control Offices in the railway stations to get ration tickets to use while at home.

By then there were calls from Britain to reduce the amount of food being given to the troops. In response, the QM of the 13/Royal Fusiliers decreed an economy campaign. He put up a notice in the reserve camp advising men to 'Eat less and save shipping'. Graffiti was added: 'Eat less and save shitting'. But the campaign did bear fruit because they became the thriftiest battalion in the division. Second Lieutenant Read saw the same notice in July 1918, painted on a lorry.

Hard Work in the Trenches

Physical toil in the trenches was a great burden on Tommy. Fatigue parties for rations, ammunition and other supplies meant work for at least half the night. There had to be constant repairs to parapets, trench walls, floors, barbed-wire defences and cables. There were also sandbags to fill with earth.

Additionally, there was sentry duty, possible patrols into No Man's Land, even raids on enemy trenches, burials of the dead, and retrieval of the wounded. The 1/Cameronians in the Ypres Salient in December 1914, in the early days of settled trench warfare, found, if they were lucky, they would get only about six hours rest in every twenty-four. It remained about the same or worse for the rest of the war. On quiet fronts there might be better days; in February 1916 Major Vignoles of the 10/Lincolns (Grimsby Pals) recorded that his men took breakfast and rum and then slept, except for sentry duty, for most of the day. They were very lucky.

But it was impossible for the experts of 1914 to foresee the demands of trench warfare on the men defending them. However, the extent of the burden of work required did become clearer in 1915 and, in view of that, the ration could have been steadily increased at that time or in 1916 with the demands of the Battle of the Somme. The U-boat campaign eventually made this well-nigh impossible in 1917.

The bitter winters of 1916/17 and 1917/18 presented an even stronger case for increased rations. In Delville Wood (Somme) on 21 January 1917, twenty-five degrees of frost was recorded and on 9 April 1917, when the offensive at Arras was launched, it was still snowing.

Sergeant Read of the 17/Leicesters (January 1917) put what was left of a loaf in his mess tin overnight to keep it from the rats and the mice. In the morning it was frozen solid. Even putting it on the stove made no difference. He was only able to defrost it by sleeping with it. David Bell, a machine-gunner, got icicles on his moustache on 13 January 1917 and his bread and cheese froze. Like Read he slept on it.

Rats

Rats were serious competitors for food. If you were trying to save anything for later you had to try and make sure the rats could not get at it. They could tear sandbags to bits and shower you with the contents as you slept and eat the food off your body, legs or face. Rats had no fear: they would attempt to eat anything, anywhere, anyhow. They were impervious to bad language and threats.

Frank Dunham reported as late as October 1917 that there was no rat poison available. Hanging up sandbags was no use because rats were adept at shinning down the string. This happened to Frank on 30 November 1916 when rats ate the contents of several parcels he had just received.

Corporal Henry Gregg of the 119 Machine-Gun Company in 1917 was trying to exterminate a persistent rat when, during the battle, it fell on another man's bread and cheese. Gregg informed his mate of this accident when he returned from sentry duty. But this bloke wasn't going to throw away perfectly good food and, on enquiring closely where the rat had actually landed, cut away the offending portion and ate the rest of it.

Good and Bad Meals

In the diaries and letters of soldiers good meals were remembered fondly in great detail, and so were rotten meals. The 1/Cameronians throughout December 1914 at Houplines in the trenches received half a gill of rum every morning (a double ration), oats or bacon for breakfast, tinned bully beef or M and V stew and potatoes for dinner, bread, butter, cheese or jam for tea, and plenty of tea or cocoa, tinned milk and sugar. Of course, at that stage of the war, they had to do their own cooking but they were quite happy about this as long as the rations kept coming.

Corporal Frederick Hodges of the 10/Lancashire Fusiliers thought his meals were 'adequate' when the rations arrived. They had bread, cheese, jam, margarine, tea and sometimes M and V and water flavoured with petrol and chloride of lime (see below). Strangely, he did not mention bully beef or biscuits.

Private Harold Horne of the Northumberland Fusiliers wrote of pork and beans, bread, hard biscuits, twelve-ounce bully beef tins, tinned jam, tinned butter, sugar and tea plus cigarettes and tobacco. Sometimes, he got Maconochie to heat over a charcoal brazier. When the cooks were nearer the trenches he got cooked meat, bacon, vegetables and puddings (when they had flour).

The rations for the 2/RWF in the Bois Grenier trenches in January 1915 were good – more bully beef than they could eat and plenty of biscuits (they didn't seem to mind this, probably because it was so early in the war). The only thing that appeared to disappoint them was a paltry bread supply.

Private Peter McGregor of the 14/Argyle and Sutherland Highlanders wrote enthusiastically to his wife in June 1915 about an excellent dinner of stew, potatoes and cabbage. Officers came round asking if there were any complaints and the CO offered McGregor a second helping. In contrast Private Clifford Carter of the 10/East Yorkshires (Hull Commercials) on 18 November 1914 had dry bread and cheese for breakfast, dry bread and cheese for dinner and cheese and dry bread for tea.

Heavy losses in the big battles often resulted in more food and drink for the survivors. Most men did not hesitate to take from their dead comrades knowing they would have been served the same way if they had been killed. Rations still arrived on the basis of the ration strength of the company until an adjustment was made. Also, parcels for dead men were shared out amongst the living in the trenches since it was seldom feasible or sensible to try and return them to the senders.

In late 1915 Private H.S. Clapham was happy sitting around a brazier consuming a meal of tea, tinned salmon and biscuits. But J.B. MacLean, also within the first year of the war, remembered cold food, above all, except tea brewed over a candle. Roast meat or bully beef was cold. There was bread, butter and jam, perhaps some sweet biscuits or tinned fruit. He found the food monotonous, especially during the winter. He longed for a meal in a warm room, on a table and with no dirt in the food or the tea. Later in the war he did get hot food in the trench, brought up in boxes packed with straw.

Private Frank ('Dick') Richards (2/RWF) in October 1914 said he was lucky to get biscuits, which was most strange. He shared a one-pound tin of bully beef with another man and a tin of jam with five others. But this jam was rotten – possibly made with marrow, and Richards hoped to meet those responsible for it and shoot them. He reckoned that any man who had enough sugar, milk and bread was one in a million or very friendly with the cooks.

Signallers for the artillery positioned in front of the trenches often fared badly for food, usually having to crawl back for it, which was sometimes not possible because of enemy action. Private John Jackson, a signaller with the 6/Cameronians, waited in the rain in vain for food from 1–3 November 1915. Eventually he waded back through waist-high water all the way to the support area two miles away. It took him hours. Hearing of his ordeal the cooks plied him with food and tea and gave him as much as he could carry to take back.

Private George Coppard, a machine-gunner of the 2/Queen's Royal West Surreys, thought that the worst items to get a share of whilst manning their posts beyond the front trenches were tins of something or other – bully beef, pork and beans, jam or butter. Some NCOs in the trenches were inclined to be cavalier about handing stuff out with the result that the poor machine-gunners lost out.

In times of deprivation, NCOs had to be more careful about ensuring that every man had a fair share of the rations. Sergeant Perry Webb (7/Dorsets) remembered doling out the exact number of biscuits to each man and the exact dollop of jam (May 1918). Henry Ogle also recalled a ration distribution. A corporal laid out the goods on a groundsheet into four parts, one for each section. Lance-corporals took the food for their section. There were tins of plum and apple jam, tins of butter, bread, cigarettes, tobacco, matches and mail.

Corporal Middleton also brought a tin of 'hard tack' (the infamous dog biscuits) to make up the iron ration packs. He warned men not to trade their bully beef for anything, including love. An imminent kit inspection would check whether their iron rations were intact. A keen officer of the 1/Hull Pals lectured his platoon (25 March 1916) about waste and ordered that every man would get his specified ration, and not a scrap more. He actually threw or poured away the smallest excess.

Fried Mule and Ostrich Eggs

There were occasional odd additions to normal rations. Smiler Marshall reckoned that one of his cooks fried up a dead mule and it tasted good (Smiler also said that he put his rum ration on his feet). The sergeant-cook of the 2/RWF found some edible snails on 23 May 1918 in Héricourt. Tommy didn't like them.

Rabbit sometimes appeared on the menu. 'The Chocolate Soldier' – General Fanshawe, or 'Fanny', gave Lieutenant Vaughan of the 1/8/Royal Warwickshires some cold, cooked rabbit on 27 August 1917. Vaughan saved some for after capturing Langemarck Ridge. The Warwicks did capture the Ridge but Vaughan's rabbit had become plastered in filthy mud and was inedible. The Army Rabbit Skin Clearing Commission marketed six million skins during the war and made £123,000, which went to Army welfare funds. Presumably, Tommy ate some of the rabbits.

In the summers, sometimes very hot, many units were supplied with neat lemon juice. Unfortunately one unit received it instead of the rum ration on a cold winter's day and there was nearly a mutiny. Puddings were always very popular but supplies of flour were often uncertain. The 2/RWF had plenty of 'spotted dick' in December 1915. The occasional meat pudding was 'a baby's head', and a large suet pudding was 'a sixty pounder'. Figs ('deaf 'uns') were a popular addition.

Captured German parcels were also an occasional supplement to rations, providing a touch of variety: Tommy didn't get a lot of German sausage, or even English sausage. A night patrol of the Hood Battalion, Royal Naval Division, jumped on a German wagon, bayoneted the driver and stole the mail, some schnapps and a box of cigars intended for a German general. The sailors handed over the cigars to their CO. A 2/RWF patrol (26 October 1914) found an enemy sniper in a haystack with a week's rations. And this was a very enterprising battalion – A Company installed a cow in the trenches on 23 October 1914. It provided a steady supply of milk until 8 November when it was hit by a shell.

Some of the early trenches in 1914 and 1915 were in the midst of fruit trees and bushes. When autumn arrived in 1915 men crept out at night and took advantage of bounteous nature – flat on their backs. By 1916 you were lucky to find a tree or a bush intact.

Wild geese and ducks sometimes flew over the trenches, attracting marksmen from both sides. A Tommy actually hit a goose on the Somme but it fell to ground in the enemy trenches. They put up a notice, 'So many thanks'.

In the hot summers dysentery abounded as bloated flies settled on food. Lieutenant Guy Chapman (13/Royal Fusiliers) had a spell in the trenches when all he could recall were these horrible flies, recurrent and nauseating stewed beef and enormous onions that even Worcester sauce or neat whisky could not overpower.

Lieutenant-Colonel E.P. Cawston suggested using boiled ostrich eggs as part of rations. His uncle owned the Cawston Ostrich Farm in Los Angeles. Hatchett's of Piccadily had bought these eggs to make a speciality of theirs – ostrich egg omelettes, but they never caught on because they were too expensive. An ostrich egg was the equivalent of twenty-four chicken eggs. It could be cut into slices and served up with some bacon. Unfortunately the British Army did not take up Cawston's interesting idea.

Rations Behind the Lines

Tommy ate much better in the rest areas and camps. The delivery of the rations was much less fraught and the cooks were always on hand. There were well-stocked canteens and soup kitchens, civilian cafés, restaurants and shops. In these places eggs were readily available and egg and chips was Tommy's favourite (Chapter Fifteen). For a minority in the rest areas there was a ration of eggs, paid for out of proceeds from the sale of Army swill.

Tommy sometimes ate so well behind the lines that rations were thrown away, especially bully beef and hard biscuits. Frank Dunham saw a lot of ration ('possessed') cheese being wasted in November 1916 at Halifax Camp near Hazebrouck. He was himself served with rare bloaters in the village of Maroeuil in October 1917 so perhaps he was also throwing cheese away at this time. Winston Groom was eating Palethorpe's sausages at Bout Deville so what he was doing with his bully beef was nobody's business.

The 1/Hull Pals (10/East Yorkshires), at their first billet in Longpré-les-Corps Saints in March 1916, were very pleased with their ration – plenty of beef, tinned jam and bread and butter. They called it an 'Army and Navy Ration', a reference to the goodies you could get from the Army and Navy Stores.

Water Supplies

There was considerable pressure on water supplies on the Western Front. In the first place, a vast Army had to share resources with civilian populations. Secondly, a lot of damage was inflicted on rivers, streams, reservoirs, lakes, ponds, springs and wells. There were many examples of civilian communities crossing swords with the military over the water supply. At Fersuelle on 25 November 1916 the locals protested to the 2/RWF about their habit of washing in a pond normally used for making cider. The Fusiliers had a limber cart stuck in the middle of it. Earlier that year (3 July) the battalion had marched to Talmes on a baking hot day and arrived very thirsty only to discover that the locals had removed all the pump handles.

It was particularly frustrating during the wet weather in trenches to be surrounded by water (like the Ancient Mariner) when it was not entirely wise to drink it. From the Mons retreat in August 1914 till the end of the war, medical officers advised against accepting local supplies or what nature had left lying about without liming it. Soldiers were threatened with Field Punishment No. 1 if they accepted water from civilians in August 1914. Typhoid or enteric problems could easily spread if they drank carelessly. The water in battalion carts was treated with chloride of lime as a matter of course. If water came from any other source it was best to boil it first, as Private Daniel Sweeney (2/Lincolns) told his parents in a letter home on 17 August 1915.

Water could be several feet deep in shell holes or ditches in wet weather. Yet in the early trenches of January 1915 the 2/RWF discovered only too frequently that bodies from the First Battle of Ypres could be in the bottom of the craters, not to mention other contaminations. Dick Richards at Arras in April 1917 noticed that some men were using a crump hole for water whilst others used it for an entirely different purpose.

The Taste of Water

This water could taste of explosives or contain pockets of poison gas, which caused unpleasant sensations in the mouth and could result in ulceration. Each shell hole seemed to have its own individual flavour, indicating a whole variety of cocktails and concoctions from dubious sources. However, what was clear was that these troops suffered from a lot of diarrhoea, boils and ulcers, exacerbated by poorly-cooked food.

Other methods were employed to extract local water. The 1/8/Royal Warwickshires, near Cappy on 9 February 1917, melted a large chunk of ice from a shell hole and used it for tea on the assumption that the cold had killed off all the bugs. It was not reported whether they were right or not. Similarly, Private Burrage of the Artists' Rifles at Cambrai on 31 December 1917 tried to melt snow in his eagerness for a drink, but found out that a large amount of snow took ages to melt and then produced very little water.

Sometimes soldiers became desperate. The early anti-gas respirator of 1915 was just a pad of cotton wool wrapped in gauze which had to be wetted by a solution of soda from a bottle issued to the troops. A thirsty Fusilier of the 2/RWF drank this soda and became very ill.

Rainwater was also used by thirsty Tommies. Albert Hay of 1/Black Watch made tea with rainwater collected in ground sheets pushed into holes in the bottom of the trench. He experimented and proved that if you kept draining from mess tin to mess tin this got rid of most of the mud. Thomas McCall, a Cameron Highlander, also collected water in a waterproof sheet stretched over the roof of a dugout. This water was the colour of stout but, with the addition of a lot of condensed milk and sugar, he made drinkable tea.

Fusilier Victor Packer of the Royal Irish Fusiliers dug holes below the sandbags on the parapet of his trench, allowing surface water to drip into a container overnight. This liquid teemed with 'little black things' but these tended to disappear when the 'water' was boiled.

Even when sufficient supplies of water were arriving from the water carts in the transport lines men sought alternative sources because they could not get used to the taste of ration water. Neither petrol nor lime was brewed out by boiling water for stews or tea. Lieutenant Sidney Rogerson retched after his first drink of tea tasting of petrol. Officers preferred to drink their whisky neat rather than mix it with ration water. It was possible to burn out the petrol fumes but the de-fumigation of millions of cans was not feasible; and buying millions of proper water cans would have cost a fortune. Much of the diarrhoea was caused by the ingestion of petrol fumes. Lieutenant Ulrich Burke of 2/Devons noted this in the days before the capture of Passchendaele when his men drank even more tea than usual. Heating the water made the chances of getting diarrhoea even worse.

The reek of chloride of lime and petrol even affected the food. Corporal Read of the 17/Leicesters was in the thick of battle at Bazentin on the Somme in August 1916 when he tucked into some cold Fray Bentos and brewed some tea. The petrol and the lime in the tea created a taste in his mouth which transferred to the food. However, he had not eaten for eighteen hours and the hunger overcame the nausea from the fumes which rose in his mouth with every mouthful. After the bully beef he gritted his teeth and took some bread and cheese as well.

Hard Going

Bringing the water ration to the trenches was no easy task. Individuals in the ration party could carry two petrol cans, one in each hand. A ration party could fetch up twenty to thirty cans in this way. A party coming

In the trench Tommy dreamed of warm evenings back in an *estaminet*. Cartoon by Bruce Bairnsfather.

up to the line south of the Menin Road in October 1917 arrived with twenty-four of its twenty-eight cans holed by shell fragments and almost empty. A party struggling in terrible conditions between Hooge crater and Glencourse Wood on 15 September 1917 were struck three times in an hour by shells.

Freezing conditions, particularly in the early months of 1916 and 1917, affected water supplies badly. A divisional report of 2 February 1917 revealed that nearly 3,000 men were getting water from two men boiling it in a small tub and pouring it into petrol cans whilst another scooped up frozen spillages and returned them to the tub.

In the Somme trenches in February 1917 the 5/Royal Warwickshires were suffering from the cold and lack of water, which was a particularly perilous situation for wounded men awaiting the stretcher-bearers. They had two jars of rum but how they wished this was water, so essential was it for a wounded man. There were none of the usual problems of 'selection' for a ration party to brave the daylight hours in the communication trench to go and fetch water: every man in the battalion volunteered for this duty.

Other Sources of Water

There were other sources of water near the front line other than water carts and shell holes. In some cases civilian sources were nearer than the water cart. The 12/East Surreys in the Ypres Salient in August 1917 used the resources of a nearby abandoned mansion. Some trenches ran through or near old farmyards with undamaged and possibly safe water supplies. H. Raymond Smith volunteered to get some from the pump of a ruined farmhouse just behind the line. He walked to where the trench sloped up to ground level. The pump was about fifty yards away by a wall of the house. He ran with a container as quietly and swiftly as possible because he was now in full view of the Germans. But as he worked the pump it squeaked loudly and bullets began to zip around him and he fell flat. All went quiet and he started pumping again from a prone position. Soon his vessel was full. But he waited for several minutes before making a dash for the trench, not easy with two gallons of water. He got safely back to the trench, spilling some of it, but there was plenty left for tea for his section.

Near Ploegsteert ('Plug Street') Wood later in 1915 Private Kenneth Garry of the Honourable Royal Artillery (an infantry unit) used a pump standing right next to a bend in the communication trench. Despite its perilous position it still worked and the Germans could not see it, a very unusual combination of circumstances. Frank Dunham also miraculously came across a natural underground spring delivering pure, clean water next to 'Fosse Way', another communication trench at the bottom of Hill 60 at Zillebeke Switch.

The 2nd Field Company, Royal Engineers, made good use of a village pond at 'Plug Street' Wood (19 June 1915). However, a solid day's pumping almost drained out the whole pond, which showed the amount of water required by the military. Luckily, there were no villagers left to complain.

A shortage of water put a premium on uses other than drinking. Some men shaved (a potentially torturous task in cold and wet trenches) by saving some hot tea, thinking that it was worth sacrificing some of their precious beverage for a decent and comfortable shave. Alfred Burrage (Artists' Rifles) complained of a permanent barber's rash. On New Year's Day 1917 Frank Dunham washed from water in a ditch in sub-zero temperatures. Lance-Corporal George Coppard and his machine-gun crew ran out of water to cool their gun (July 1917) so they urinated on it. The gun subsequently worked but gave off an offensive odour.

Water Behind the Lines

A shortage of water was also not uncommon behind the lines, especially on marches away from or to the front. In these circumstances men had to rely on what was in the water carts. In hot weather the amount of water available could create serious problems for marching men with very heavy loads – sometimes in the region of thirty-five kilos. When the Connaught Rangers marched in June 1917 men were ordered to drink sparingly from the bottle on their right hips at the periodic stops, and were banned completely from taking gulps as they strode along. If they ran out before reaching the billets they were in serious trouble.

Even casualty clearing stations could run out of water. This was what happened at the large St Jean Station just outside Ypres on 6 August 1917.

Dying men had nothing to drink all day whilst 109 Field Ambulance scouted around desperately for fresh supplies.

In rest areas there was more chance of getting clean water, like from the large well with its winding gear at Fonquevillers. In December 1915 this provided all the water for the 7/Royal Warwickshires' cooks. Battalion water carts had priority on local sources but MOs still insisted on treating it before any man used it. Of course, the compensation in rest areas was that there were plenty of other types of liquid refreshment available. It could just be lemonade for teetotallers, or 'bun wallahs'. However, this was preferable to the 'brownish' water with a funny smell on tap at 2nd Lieutenant Blacker's (4/Coldstream Guards) farm billet in the winter of 1915.

Eight

Bread and Breakfast

Supplying Bread

The bread ('rooty') ration for front-line trenches at the outset of the war was eighteen ounces a day, just over half a two-pound loaf. This was reduced to sixteen ounces in 1917. Fresh(ish) bread was another morale-booster for the troops. One of the first questions asked as the ration party arrived was: 'How many to a bun?'

As with supplies generally the arrival of bread was prey to many factors – enemy action, the weather, and especially the availability of flour. For instance, there were reports in the winter of 1916 that dried, ground turnip was sometimes used as a substitute.

French bakers had similar problems but Tommy was able to supplement his bread ration from this source in the rest areas and perhaps take some back to the trenches to last him a day or two. However, local bread was often too expensive, especially by 1916, when shortages of flour became acute. Private Ernest Parker remembered the intoxicating aroma of baking bread in the *boulangerie* in Vignacourt early in 1916, and the frustration of knowing he could not afford to buy any. To make matters worse, during the winter of 1916 the French government banned the sale of bread to British soldiers in order to give priority to their own troops and civilians.

The Bread Ration

The amount received by Tommy varied enormously; however, the ration seemed generous to men transferring from service in the Middle East. When the 10/East Yorkshires arrived in March 1916 and the Royal Marine Light Infantry Brigade in May 1916 they had not seen bread for months. To Horace Bruckshaw of the Marines, half a loaf was heaven. Sadly, by 25 June he was getting none again.

The bread ration in the rest areas was slightly less than that for the front, but the evidence suggests very strongly that Tommy actually did much better there than in the front line because of supply difficulties. If the bread was going to take a long time to get there it was a waste of time and money to send it up, and therefore it was handed out behind the lines. Moreover, Tommy could buy more from French bakers until late in 1916. In a sense, Tommy was prepared to wait until he got to the back areas to have a feast of fresh bread. But he was up at the front for a fortnight at a time and if bread was not forthcoming after a few days he was really missing it and cursing the 'dog' biscuits.

The 7/Dorsets had very little bread throughout April and May 1918 during the major German offensive. My father grumbled because his daily loaf was reduced to a half at this time, but he was really lucky to get any. In fact, the ration was more likely to be 'three men to a bun' when it was getting through. That was what Frank Dunham (25/Londons) was getting in November 1916. Right at the beginning of the war men of the 2/RWF received a quarter of a loaf a day, and so did the 17/Leicesters in 1915, both in rest areas, due to disruption caused by bad weather.

The ration was not met sometimes because the suppliers had not taken into account new drafts of men to a battalion. Mind you, the reverse happened when there were a lot of casualties and bread was sent up to meet the official ration strength; the survivors probably got their half a loaf until HQ adjusted the figures.

Lieutenant Roe wrote that for a long time early in the war his platoon of sixty men had one loaf a week each, three and a half times below the ration. In a letter home in April 1915 Private Braid, in the midst of complaining about the food generally, calculated that he got one ounce of bread a day, about one slice. The 25/Londons did worse in December 1914 – one loaf for thirty-two men. They cut cards and the four with the highest had a quarter of a loaf each. However, by 1918 the troops generally began to get more bread than people at home.

When they could get local bread it was an absolute delight. Private Henry Ogle of the 7/Royal Warwickshires was in Houchin in July 1915. At the local *boulangerie* there were all sorts of loaves – long, twisted ones, straight ones and curved ones with an open ring or tongue. He watched villagers buy enormous black rye loaves which they cut with a special type of scythe as they held the bread under their armpits. But soldiers found that the trouble with the cheap rye bread was that it soon went stale (probably why the locals ate it on their way home). Also, it was pretty horrible without butter or margarine. The Old Contemptibles came across 'siege' bread in Le Havre in August 1914 and found it even more disgusting. Gunner Saville Williams of the Royal Horse Artillery reportedly paid eleven francs for a white loaf there on the 18th. He must have had a lot of cash to spare – this was about ten days' basic pay for a Tommy.

At the other end of the war, when the 4/Coldstream Guards captured Mauberge in November 1918, the local ladies came out with lots of superb white bread and cakes. They had been saving up flour just for this occasion.

'Pozzy'

The jam ('pozzy') ration was usually spread on the bread, or a biscuit if there was no bread. Jam and biscuit was sometimes boiled into a hash. Five or six men usually shared a tin or carton of jam. Private Williams of the 2/East Surreys fondly recalled the day in August 1917 when he had the luxury of a whole tin to himself after a scrounging expedition had ended very successfully. They spread it on thick that day.

The only trouble with jam was that Tommy mainly got plum and apple jam made by Tommy Tickler's (a Yorkshire firm).

Tickler's Jam, Tickler's Jam.
How I love old Tickler's Jam.
Plum and Apple in a one-pound pot,
Sent from Blighty in a ten-ton lot.

Tommy was liable to get even more of it in his parcels: Private Syd Baker of the 238 Machine-Gun Company, sitting in a trench with its walls strengthened by layers of unopened Tommy Tickler's plum and apple jam, got some from his wife. Tommy Tickler's turned men into poets. Gilbert Frankau wrote in *The Wipers Times* of 13 March 1916:

> No human force could hope to dam
> Those waves of Plum and Apple Jam.

A song was sung to the tune of 'A Wee Deock an' Doris':

> Plum and Apple,
> Apple and Plum.
> Plum and Apple,
> There is always some.
> The ASC get strawberry jam
> And lashings of rum.
> But we poor blokes
> We only get
> Apple and Plum.

But when Lance-Corporal Vic Cole of the 1/Queen's Own Royal West Kents was lying miserably in a water-filled shell hole near the Menin Road on 20 September 1917, strafed by enemy planes, the only food he had was his tin of T.T.'s plum and apple. It tasted really good. Ironically, it was labelled 'strawberry jam'. You could do a lot worse than Tommy Tickler's – gooseberry and rhubarb or marrow.

But there was better jam than Tommy Tickler's, even if it was still plum and apple. Harry Patch of the 10/Duke of Cornwall's had some very nice stuff made by Crosse and Blackwell. In the Bickersteth Diaries there is mention of an officer writing home on 30 May 1915 for some 'Tiptree Farm' jam.

On 25 March 1918 Private Doug Roberts (7/Buffs East Kent) was sitting in a trench when a shell landed right by him. He was miraculously unhurt but he saw that Private Pierce was badly wounded. His face was just a mass of blood. Actually, it was plum and apple jam, probably Tommy Tickler's. Pierce had been eating from a tin of it. He was also unhurt. His mates probably licked him. A similar thing happened to Private Bishop of the 1/8/Royal Warwickshires on 16 August 1917 when a piece of shrapnel hit the jam in his haversack. They thought he was a gonner.

The Wonder of Breakfast

Breakfast was a special meal in the trenches. At dawn, men had just 'stood down' from night duty and could hopefully look forward to something a bit more civilised – the smell of frying bacon, the first cuppa of the day and the rum ration. Quiet fronts tended to have an unofficial truce at breakfast time: Tommy could see the wisps of blue smoke rising from the enemy's breakfast, possibly also against orders (there was more chance of Tommy's smoke being seen because the morning sun was behind the Germans). Dick Richards reckoned his fire in Polygon Wood on 26 September 1917 emitted no more smoke than a cigarette. On less quiet fronts, however, some 'morning hate' might come whizzing over. In the Givenchy trenches in the summer of 1915 a mortar bomb blew a 2/RWF breakfast to smithereens. Dick Richards lost one or two breakfasts this way. Poison gas could turn bacon green.

Some Memorable Breakfasts

Almost as popular as bacon was bacon fat. 'Roll up for your dip!' called the cooks (if they were there). Private Alfred Bromfield remembered very clearly on 22 April 1915 standing in the trench cooking 'his little bit of breakfast'. His chief interest in those days was fried bacon with fried cheese. He had saved up a couple of rashers for about three days in the lid of his mess tin. He placed the cooked bacon on a slice of bread, chopped up the cheese very finely and dropped it into the bacon fat and added a little water so that it wouldn't stick. He cooked this till it bubbled and added it to the bread and bacon. It was his speciality.

The 17/Leicesters went to the trenches in August 1915 to learn the ropes from a Fusilier battalion who had managed to get some fresh eggs: the Leicesters helped them to collect some dry sticks and some big stones to make a small fire. A mess tin lid was the frying pan, and eggs, bacon and fried bread were soon sizzling away. It looked like the best breakfast of all time for the Leicesters, until a rifle grenade landed on the meal. But it took the brunt of the blast and no one was hurt.

Second Lieutenant J.S. Tatham of the 9/King's Royal Rifle Corps, in the trenches in January 1916, remembered that his breakfasts during that spell in the front line were as good as anything he got in the rest areas – essentially porridge, eggs and bacon. Lieutenant Spicer (9/King's Own Yorkshire Light Infantry), at Loos in October 1915, had breakfasts so tasty they tended to have the same meal for lunch and dinner as well.

Corporal Read of the 17/Leicesters liked welsh rarebit – cheese melted in a mess tin lid on bread toasted on the end of a bayonet. However, when he was at Guedecourt on the Somme in September 1916 he had to make do with a cold rasher on bread, and tea brewed on a tiny fire built with wood chippings. He had filled his pockets with these when at rest. Private Gary's speciality was his version of 'café au lait' – cocoa with some milk added.

Perhaps breakfast was better when the cooks weren't in the trenches because Tommy had to wait longer for his food when they were there. The cooks had to contend with a small brazier or stove cooking perhaps for a platoon of sixty-four men, sometimes short of fuel or contending with damp fuel. Tommy could do no more whilst waiting but tuck into some bread and jam. However, the cooks could make it worth the wait. Corporal George Coppard and his pals had a nice surprise on 19 November 1917 waiting for the Cambrai battle to kick off. No fires were allowed and there was no smoking. Their suffering was relieved by the unexpected arrival of a field kitchen and porridge and lovely, steaming tea.

Sausages sometimes made an appearance, usually from tins and usually only for officers. Lieutenant-Colonel Eberle of the 2nd Field Company, Royal Engineers, ate sausages and bacon off a sandbag table in the trench in Ploegsteert Wood (16 April 1915). Also, on the 24th, he had breakfast in an infantry major's dugout – tongue, marmalade on bread and tea.

Nine

Food and Drink During the Big Offensives

'Rabbits'

The remark made by an officer back on 16 March 1915 had a pro-phetic ring about it. Sitting in a company dugout in the trenches at Bois Grenier he compared himself to a rabbit: munching, then stopping when a noise was heard, pausing to see where it landed, and, if it didn't land on you, munching again. That was the sort of existence endured in the offensives of 1916 and 1917 – the Somme, Arras, the Third Battle of Ypres and Cambrai. All these campaigns were preceded by many days of bombardment and counter-bombardment. Then Tommy went over the top, over the bags, over the parapet to advance on the enemy. He was no longer a rabbit in a hole being shot at, he was a rabbit in an open field being shot at.

On the first day of the Battle of the Somme, 1 July 1916, the 'Black Day' of the British Army, about 20,000 men were killed. It didn't seem so bad waiting in the trench when the rations had arrived safely, despite the German counter-bombardment. Lieutenant Richard Hawkings of the 11/Royal Fusiliers had a good breakfast and handed out a packet of Woodbines to each of his men. But in another trench Major Jack of the 2/Cameronians had only tea and bread and butter for breakfast, the more solid of the rations having been destroyed by enemy shelling during the night. Good luck, bad luck – that's how it was when they went over the top. Captain Billy Nevill famously gave his company some footballs to dribble towards the enemy trenches, with a prize for the man who kicked the first ball into one of them. Billy perished immediately.

James Jack survived but not the CO of 1/Hampshires, who lay mortally wounded in a hole and said to the Tommy lying beside him, 'If you knows of a better hole, go to it', the immortal caption on one of Bruce Bairnsfather's cartoons.

The Somme – Deprivation and Surprises

By the third day of the battle Siegfried Sassoon was bemoaning the lack of oranges – as remote as a sunset. Gunner Leonard Ounsworth was more concerned with the lack of bread and butter, jam, tea and sugar. Then it all suddenly arrived and everyone had double the normal amount of food because half the company had gone. Dick Richards (2/RWF) took two tins of Maconochie and half a loaf from a dead comrade in High Wood. The RSM's batman of this battalion was killed in the communication trench and he had with him the RSM's rations, but everyone save the RSM had some of them. Lance-Corporal Henry Ogle (7/Royal Warwickshires) found bags of sweet biscuits and real ground coffee made from roasted malt (none of your ersatz) in a German trench. There was also a tin of very sticky lemon marmalade which gave Ogle a tremendous thirst when he ate the lot (Pozières).

Lance-Corporal Ernest Parker (10/Durham Light Infantry) found cigars and tins of mixed butter and jam in another German trench. This battalion was later decimated between Guedecourt and Delville Wood on 16 September. Parker, one of the few survivors, had a whole tin of butter to himself, like the rest of the men who survived, and they all could eat as many tins of beans as they liked. Meanwhile, George Coppard (37 Machine-Gun Company) was in 'Whizz-Bang Villa' serving up three bully beef rissoles to each of his crew, with potatoes fried in bacon fat, followed by stewed fruit. Every now and then a bullet crashed off one of the walls.

The Somme provided good evidence of what a big battle could do to the bacon ration. Throughout the whole of July the 2/RWF had a piece of bacon half the size of a packet of Woodbines. In fact, some of the Fusiliers preferred to dip their bread in the bacon fat instead of taking such a short rasher.

On 7 July, during an attack on Contalmaison, provisions sent for the 11/South Wales Borderers suffered severe losses. There were fifty-two men in Sergeant Albert Perryman's charge and he received one and a half

loaves of bread, a piece of boiled bacon covered in mud, a few hard biscuits, some currants and sultanas and one petrol tin full of tea. One of his
lads said to him, 'Say, Sarn't, the buggers don't intend us to die on a full
stomach, do they?' Perryman was very upset that his brave men had so
little to eat. 'Anyone would think I'm Jesus Christ,' he muttered fiercely,
'with the loaves and the fish – there ain't no fish, neither.' The section
corporals drew lots and the winning section took all the food.

Withdrawal to the Hindenburg Line

In the early months of 1917 the Germans staged a planned withdrawal
to the heavily fortified Hindenburg Line north and east of the Somme
battlefield. This created a unique stage of the war as the retreating
Germans played cat and mouse with the cautiously advancing British.
They destroyed whole villages so that the British could not use any of the
resources being vacated. Thousands of fruit trees and telegraph poles were
cut down. Booby traps were set everywhere. It was more in this stage of
the war than any other that the lingering brotherhood of man illustrated
in the Christmas Truce of 1914 was finally laid to rest. At Nurlu the 2/
West Yorkshires used an abandoned stove. Later, troops coming across it
found gun cotton inserted into the wall behind it. How it didn't blow up
was a miracle.

Arras – April 1917

Food was hard to come by during this engagement. Gunner Philip
Sylvester of the Royal Artillery existed on mouldy biscuits, discarded
mud-covered crusts of bread and turnips for several days. Sergeant Read
(17/Leicesters) had no proper meal and no hot drink for over a week.
His Tommy Cooker had run out of fuel and there was no wood for a fire.
Meanwhile, Captain Spicer of 9/King's Own Yorkshire Light Infantry
complained about the lack of an oven or any eggs. Dick Richards was
without any food or drink for a day and searched the packs of the dead.
He found half a loaf of bread, some biscuits and two bottles of water.

Three starving scarecrow-like Tommies of a Dorset battalion had been
prisoners of the Germans for three months, doing forced labour with

The ingredients of Army soup varied. Reproduced by kind permission of Leo Cooper.

very little food. They were allowed to escape and managed to stagger to the Arras front line opposite an Australian battalion. They were lucky not to have been shot. Within a few minutes the Aussies had produced steaming hot tea and handed over anything tasty from their packs.

Third Battle of Ypres

The prelude to the battle was the attack on the ridges at Messines, south of the Salient, to gain high ground. The ridge was blown off by a million tons of TNT on 7 June 1917. The 2/RWF remembered this day because one of them dropped and smashed his bottle of HP Sauce, and reserves coming up the communication trench were met by this familiar and tasty smell which overcame the reek of mustard gas and phosgene.

As the 2/West Yorkshires awaited the order to leave their trenches on the first day of the battle, they had a good meal before midnight (30 July 1917) and tea, bread and butter in the early hours of the 31st. At the same time, Lieutenant Vaughan (1/8/Royal Warwickshires) was ready to lead his men over Bridge 2A of the Yser Canal just north of Ypres. The cooks brought up the field kitchens very near the assault troops and provided lots of good food during the night. Vaughan himself had sizzling hot bacon and sausages. Officers of the 2/Lancashire Fusiliers, also waiting on the 30th, had bacon, eggs and tinned sausages for breakfast, steak, potatoes, beans and sweet omelettes for lunch, tea, bread and jam in the late afternoon and steak, potatoes and tinned fruit and custard for dinner.

The 12/East Surreys had regular meals in August during the battle and full rations of rum. Then came a day with nothing to eat or drink. The next day bread and jam covered in mud arrived but again there was nothing to drink. Volunteers went back to see what they could scrounge and Private Williams returned with a lot of bread and several tins of jam.

In the struggle for Poelcappelle Captain Philip Berliner, of the 2/7/ Londons, under severe bombardment in a trench, received an urgent call from D Company HQ to send on 351688 Private Blount's false teeth, which he had left behind in the trench. He must have been having difficulty eating the biscuits.

Passchendaele

In the thick of the last assaults on Passchendaele Ridge, men became isolated from their units in the wild, battle-scarred terrain. It wasn't trench warfare any more, just a wild scramble between the shell holes in thick, liquid mud. A machine-gunner, David Thomas Ferguson, searched frantically for food and drink beyond Irish Farm towards Crown Prince Farm and at last found two tins floating in a crump hole. One was full of cold soup and the other full of rum, and this combination kept him going, rather unsteadily, until he found his way back to his unit.

Machine-gunners in outlying posts and stretcher-bearers searching for wounded men were particularly at risk of separation. Frank Dunham, after he had carried dozens of men back to the aid post, wandered around for a day without food or drink but luckily stumbled across a labour company who gave him some of what little food they had. In a hole near St Julien, Lieutenant Vaughan ate rain-soaked bread and cheese impregnated with the fibres of sandbags and drank cold tea. At least he had some cigarettes and whisky left.

One of the best accounts of the final days of the assault on Passchendaele is by Alfred McLelland Burrage, a short story writer who had joined the Artists' Rifles ('Ex-Private X' was his pen name). For more than twenty-four hours on 30–31 October 1917 he was part of a decoy attack allowing the Canadians to the south to drive up the Ridge. Accompanied by a battalion of the Bedfordshires (these two battalions were almost all of what was left of the British Army in this sector), they were decimated amidst the wild and wet terrain by the German artillery.

Burrage was one of the few survivors of this doomed attack. He ate by rifling through the packs of dead men. He spent the night in a wrecked ex-German dugout, waist deep in water and surrounded by the dead and dying. He had to drink a little of the disgusting water lying about, just a few drops in thirty-six hours to keep him alive. A drink made from coffee cubes in an aid post on 1 November was truly life-saving. As he rejoined what was left of his battalion the QMS gave him a mess tin three-quarters full of rum.

Cambrai

The first massed tank attack of the war took place on 20 November 1917 at Cambrai. Corporal George Coppard, waiting to operate his machine-gun post, had good porridge for breakfast. Subsequently, he ate iron rations for three days – bully beef, biscuits, meat extract and a little tea and sugar. Before these three days were up he ran out of water and lasted another twenty-four hours without a drink.

The Germans were driven back several miles by the tanks, yet by the end of the month had recovered most of the lost ground (and gained some). The weather became colder and colder. This was when Alfred Burrage tried to melt snow for water. As the year neared its end he found a very comfortable, warm and friendly dugout housing a section responsible for bringing up ammunition from dumps behind the lines. The cocoa there was the best he had tasted, due to what his new friends put in it.

On the last day of the year there was a surprise attack, and Burrage, then a stretcher-bearer, got lost. One unit thought Burrage was wounded because he was covered in blood. Actually, it came from one of the men he had brought in. They showered him with tea, cigarettes, and lots of bread, butter and jam. He wandered on, half dead with fatigue, and now in agony with trench foot. A bottle with some whisky in it kept him going but eventually he collapsed. He was picked up and taken to a casualty clearing station and then to England with a Blighty One. He returned in 1918.

Ten

Parcels

The Parcel Industry

The dispatch of parcels from Britain to the Western Front was an industry in itself. By the middle of 1915 the British Forces Post Office was handling 60,000–70,000 parcels a day through Le Havre. In the week before Christmas 1915 there were 300,000–500,000 parcels a day. Six special trains and four special boats were added to the normal transport to take care of the extra loads and a temporary sorting centre was set up in Regent's Park. A total of 300,000 parcels a day was standard by 1917.

In 1915 there was a campaign to reduce the cost of sending parcels from the foreign to the inland rate. This was refused by the Postmaster General on the grounds that the service wouldn't be able to handle the volume of parcels which would result from a reduced postage. There was a weight limit of seven pounds on each parcel. One parcel which was sent to Captain Billy Nevill cost the equivalent of Tommy's weekly pay.

The number of parcels received by some soldiers, especially officers, was remarkable. John Glubb may have exaggerated a little when he recorded that he got about six a day during one spell, but he was not prone to inaccuracy. John Reith had one every two or three days in 1914. Captain Eric Fairtlough thanked his mother on 4 November 1914 for parcel number seven. The Royal Fusiliers were known as 'The Chocolate Soldiers' because they had so many parcels.

The Service

It was generally a very efficient service as long as there was no trouble from U-boats in the English Channel or bad weather or hold-ups on the railways and roads. A parcel could be posted in Piccadilly late on Thursday and be in the hands of the recipient on Saturday afternoon. On the other hand, they could take four or five days. When you consider that all that was written on them was a Tommy's name and unit the BFPO did a pretty good job.

There was some theft in transit. In January 1916 the 13/Royal Fusiliers were driven out of their billets by a fire and when they got back all their parcels had disappeared. Len Beechey of the 13/East Yorkshires got a parcel from home which was damaged and some dates were missing. A pie looked like it had been hit by a whizz-bang but it still tasted good. To avoid this sort of tampering bogus labels were often put on parcels. Dick Richards' whisky was labelled 'sauce'. The label 'Army Temperance Society Publications' indicated expensive cigars.

What Was in the Parcels?

Some of the food and drink in officers' parcels was extremely expensive: the staple of Billy Nevill's was cigars and brandy. Private Frank Bass (9/Norfolks) got a tin of peaches, a loaf (hopefully delivered quickly) and butter, fish paste, tobacco and chocolate, plus a sleeping helmet, a pair of socks and a towel.

When parcels accumulated at billets in Septmonts (it was sometimes impossible to get them to the trenches), during the advance to the Aisne in October 1914, it looked like a miniature Harrods when they had been opened. Stuart Dolden's battalion came back from Loos to Hulluch in 1915 and seventy bags of parcels awaited them. Around Christmas time in 1915 the 1/Cameronians in Armentières received seasonal offerings – plum puddings, mince pies and a lot of tobacco. Captain James Jack got oatcakes, shortcakes and foie gras.

Letters of requests from soldiers give some idea of the range of food and drink in parcels. Private Jack Clapham (3 July 1915) was short of sugar and also wanted a tin of cocoa. Second Lieutenant H.M. Stanford wanted Carlyle tobacco and wooden safety matches (7 November 1914).

An officer of the 9/East Surreys asked for cakes and sweets 'of the hard nature'. An officer called Hakewell-Smith was keen on a dozen kippers, Savory and Moore's special sausages and also their very nice chocolates. Captain Rose was hoping for ham, cake, sardines, sweets and chocolate, as well as Needles Army Fruit Tablets, cherry whisky, sloe gin, café au lait and cocoa. Char Beechey of the 8/Royal Fusiliers requested a mustard tin full of dripping (cooked meat fat to put on bread) to liven up his toast (letter of 15 November 1916). He wrote again on 9 December to say how much he had enjoyed it. Len Beechey wanted lime juice tablets (7 February 1917) and got them – these were popular amongst soldiers aware of the dangers of vitamin deficiency.

The troops did thank their donors profusely (at the same time usually asking for more). Len Beechey wrote on 6 May 1917 to say thanks for honey. Private George Adams thanked his mother for the cake he had received but asked that in future she separated it from the soap.

Confectionery was very much in demand to sweeten up Tommy's existence. Private Daniel Sweeney (2/Lincolns) gave thanks for his butterscotch and chocolates (22 August 1915). Billy Nevill did very well for sweets, including 'Hastings Hun Poison', which was home-made coconut ice, and peppermint creams. Bulls' eyes were much in demand because they were hard and lasted a long time. Items like this were not generally available in canteens or French or Flemish shops. This was also true of special items such as Easter eggs. Harold Beechey, preparing for the Battle of Arras in April 1917, sent home thanks for some.

John Reith received a splendid box of candy from a girl he had never met (and never did meet). She and some friends had each chosen a soldier from a picture in a Glasgow newspaper to send parcels to. She sent parcels regularly after that. Many soldiers received gift parcels from well-wishers they didn't know. Sergeant J. Hancock of the 1/Royal Fusiliers was adopted as her 'front line champion' by Amy Griffiths of St John's School, Isle of Dogs, East London. She sent him tobacco and cigarettes. Bernard Livermore was sent cake by his old dairyman and 'dainties'. Len Beechey (18/Irish Rifles) was the lucky recipient of enormous chocolate creations. His favourite was the 'three-cornered things' (letter of 9 April 1917).

Parcels came in particularly handy when rations were short. Frank Dunham was getting a slice of bread a day at the aid post near Havrincourt on 7 December 1917 when a good parcel arrived. Horace Bruckshaw (Royal Marines Light Infantry) was in a similar plight when he arrived back late in the day (10 July 1916) from a bombing course and found there was no dinner left. He'd also missed out on breakfast. But then he was handed a parcel containing a delicious cake.

In the terrible weather of January 1917 parcels were more welcome than ever. You can imagine the feelings of Len Beechey, struggling to get water from a frozen stream, as he opened a package to reveal potted meat, sweet biscuits, shortbread (his favourite) and sandwich cake (his second favourite).

In cold weather Oxo was especially life-saving. Rifleman Perry Jones was making some for Captain Whitmore when it became dark and fires normally had to be extinguished. However, the good captain wanted his Oxo so much he didn't give the order to put it out. Jones, aware of the risks of fire at night, covered the fire with a waterproof sheet and crawled underneath to blow on the embers. He came out looking like 'a smoked haddock', but the Oxo was fantastic.

Too Many Parcels

In 1917 many troops, especially the officers, felt they were getting too much from home in view of the shortages there, but the reason why Private Peter McGregor (14/Argyll and Sutherland Highlanders) asked his Granny (letter of 31 August 1916) not to send so much oatmeal was because it was too heavy to carry around. In June 1916 some Royal Fusiliers actually had a moan when some parcels arrived just as they were going up to the front because they had to carry them.

By this time Billy Nevill was getting more than he could eat or even give away (apart from Nestlé's milk butter and his beloved cigars). When he got one parcel which cost seven shillings and sixpence to send, he wrote home to say it was too much and offered to pay. Len Beechey (letter of 18 February 1917) suggested he shouldn't get any more parcels because of the scarcity of food at home and the cost of the parcels themselves.

Sharing Parcels

Tommy and his officers were great sharers: for instance, if you got a parcel with a pipe, preserved cherries, chocolate, 'gentlemen's relish' and processed cheese you probably kept the pipe, the cheese and the relish, shared the cherries with your best mate and the chocolates with all of your mates. Tommies would even share out with men they didn't know if they were short of food. After the Battle of Loos in September 1915 Stuart Dolden was in a billet when a new draft arrived from Rouen. They had been on short rations for days so Dolden and his pals gave them all their unopened parcels.

Men of the 1/8/Royal Warwickshires shared hard-boiled eggs (the senders were clearly confident that the parcels would get to their destination quickly), cheap cigars and cigarettes with a platoon officer. Second Lieutenant Arthur Gibbs (1/Welsh Guards) sent a request for more 'Bivouac' cocoa and beef tea squares, adding that if he couldn't eat it all he would share it out with his men. Whilst Lieutenant J.S. Tatham (9/King's Royal Rifle Corps) played cards with some of his platoon he shared out some cold pheasant. It was the first time they had tasted 'This 'ere sort of bird, sir'. Lieutenant R.C. Hopkinson even shared his Fortnum and Mason cake but one man suggested that the rich plum cake from the Army and Navy Stores was better.

Private Harry Patch (Duke of Cornwall's Light Infantry) received parcels about once a fortnight – an ounce of tobacco, two packets of twenty cigarettes, some sweets (if they could be scrounged, this being 1917 when sugar was short) and a few cakes. He shared the tobacco with another pipe smoker and the cigarettes equally with the three other members of his Lewis gun team – thirteen each and they took turns to have the odd one – fair shares for all.

Soldiers got so used to generous handouts from friends they would be as anxious as the recipient to know when the next lot was going to arrive. When George Coppard shared around a parcel intended for a dead comrade he subsequently wrote to the sender, the man's sister, to explain what had happened. As a result of this, the lady in question, who was called Mary, kept sending parcels to him. He shared them all so that the frequent enquiry he got was, 'I wonder when we'll get the next parcel from Mary'.

Officers shared around their goodies in the officers' mess. Billy Nevill handed around haddock from a fish basket (that had to get to the Western Front very quickly), not a bone in it. But he didn't hand around his 'Kate and Sidney' pudding which he sniffed for three days before eating.

However, you wouldn't include people you didn't like. Robert Graves remembered having some of the contents of Captain Thomas's Fortnum and Mason hampers, and the second in command of the battalion hanging around in the hope of getting something. But he was well and truly shunned. His nickname was 'Buzz Off'.

The Exotic Stuff

Some officers came from wealthier families than Billy Nevill. Captain Watson-Smyth was a company commander in the 4/Coldstream Guards and he entertained other company commanders with the contents of his magnificent parcels in 1918 at Bienvillers – the best hare, tongue, foie gras, cakes, biscuits, assorted chocolates and other delicacies. It was reckoned he got a parcel in every post.

Major Fielding (3/Coldstream Guards) had four parcels on 8 May 1916 containing two superb meat pies, a cake, foie gras, plovers' eggs and smoked salmon. Some of the more notable gifts in Billy Nevill's packages were the cigars from Maunders and some from Woolworth's to asphyxiate the flies. He favoured Ideal Milk (unsweetened) from Fortnum and Mason. He was a regular recipient of their hampers.

Siegfried Sassoon was sent a box of kippers twice a month from his Aunt Evelyn, as well as some Devon Creams. Lieutenant Guy Chapman, 13/Royal Fusiliers, ordered a case of wine – six Paul Ruinart, six Pichon Longueville, some good champagne and some of the 'velvety' curaçoa. It was sent for in April 1916 and arrived in June.

Many officers brought their own delicacies on returning from leave. Sassoon came back with some excellent salmon and two bottles of old brandy. Burgess Bickersteth of 1/Royal Dragoons brought ham, tongue and pheasant.

Hampers and Gifts

Fortnum and Mason's and the Army and Navy Stores in London sent over hundreds of parcels and hampers every day along with other food and drink purveyors and 'hundreds of emporia from Jermyn Street to Arkwright's corner shop', as Richard Holmes put it. Lieutenant Roe described F and M's parcels as being of excellent quality, very well packed in order to survive the potentially hazardous journey from Piccadily.

In addition, countless 'comforts committees' organised the dispatch of a stream of parcels to local men. So 'The Huntley Lasses' served the Gordon Highlanders. Amy Beechey's kitchen in Avondale Street, Lincoln, was a scene of constant feverish activity as she and her family and friends prepared parcel after parcel. Len Beechey (letter of 13 March 1917) was highly impressed with his sister's skilful packing – each piece of pasty snugly fitting into its tissue paper 'like a chaffinch in a nest'. It was very apparent that a lot of loving care went into this work. National newspapers also engaged in fund-raising campaigns and sent over many thousands of parcels.

Royalty played its part: Queen Alexandra gift parcels were sent out in July 1917 (she headed a 'Field Force Fund'), principally containing warm clothing and toiletries, although the box of matches came in very handy for cooking. Princess Mary distributed pretty brass boxes in January 1915 containing cigarettes, tobacco and a pipe.

After action on 19 July 1916 on the Somme the 17/Leicesters returned to Méricourt, where more than two-thirds of the parcels awaiting them were unclaimed. Alfred Burrage complained that officers had first claim on these packages in Poperinghe in November 1917 after the heroics at Passchendaele. One mother sent her son a twenty-first birthday cake but he was killed before this day. His section could not bring themselves to eat it but another platoon was not so fussy.

One Tommy was about to tuck into a nice tin of strawberries in August 1917 when he was hit on the leg by a piece of shrapnel. It was a quintessential Blighty One – nothing too horrific but enough to get him to England, at least for a spell. He took his tin of strawberries with him as a memento of his good fortune.

Eleven

Canteens

Variety

Establishments where Tommy could buy food and drink ranged from the substantial Expeditionary Force (EF) canteens to one-man enterprises in holes just behind the front line. At the beginning of the war there was official scepticism about this type of support. Lord Kitchener's response to a suggestion about canteens in 1914 was 'this war is not going to be a picnic'. Indeed, no canteens were authorised in 1914. There was a 'Field Force Canteen' in the reserve area behind Ypres very late in the year but the first EF canteen was opened early in 1915. Later in the war regiments and battalions opened their own canteens.

E.W. Hornung, who wrote the 'Raffles' books, opened up a hole in the ground in a chalk bank of a sunken road a few hundred yards behind the front near Arras to dispense hot, sweet tea. He was happiest when under fire like the men he was serving. Talbot House in Poperinghe was a nice town house rented from a wealthy businessman. Lady Egerton's Coffee House in Rouen was in a large, sturdy wooden hut and Lady Angela Forbes and her assistants worked from several wooden huts by the base camp in Étaples. Elsewhere, marquees, tents, casements, cellars and tunnels and even ex-German gun emplacements housed canteens.

There were more modest canteens than the big Army ones, usually run by religious or philanthropic organisations, such as the Salvation Army, the Church Army and the YMCA. At Étaples, in addition to Lady Forbes's huts, were the huts of the Anabaptists and Wesleyans.

Alfred Burrage of the Artists' Rifles was forced to choose between the Anabaptists' tinned salmon sandwiches and the Wesleyans' sardine sandwiches.

Len Beechey (18/London Irish) described myriad establishments within reach of the camp he was resting in March 1917. There were 'wet' (alcohol sold) and 'dry' (non-alcoholic) EF canteens in the camp. A ten-minute walk would get you to a new YMCA canteen, and yet another one forty minutes' walk away and also another EF canteen.

Coffee Stalls and Soup Kitchens

Wherever it was likely that a lot of Tommies would congregate in large numbers there was always somewhere to get a hot drink. When the train taking the Artists' Rifles to the front in March 1917 halted at a level crossing near Hesdin, coffee appeared from a small hut. Bedraggled and exhausted men, stumbling away from their fortnight at the front line, were likely to encounter a coffee stall or a soup kitchen. The soup might be of doubtful pedigree but it was hot and comforting: a 'correspondent' for *The Wipers Times* suggested that this soup might contain dead Germans, well-scraped bone and turnip tops.

Henry Allingham well recalled the sight of men staggering out of the line in a terrible state, crawling like hermit crabs covered in slime, humping great packs weighing around thirty-five kilos and at the end of their tether. All they wanted to do was sleep. Then someone in a Salvation Army hut called out 'cup of tea?' A little further down the road a Church Army worker enquired 'Cup of tea? One penny, please'. Such places restored in Tommy the will to live. George Coppard owed his survival to church canteens, in his opinion. Not only was there the coffee or tea or cocoa, but you could talk to the people running these places about your feelings, your family, problems and fears. E. W. Hornung, in his hole near Arras, encouraged the men to talk about their homes. The reason he was there was that his son, an officer in the 4/Coldstream Guards, had been killed nearby. To him his mission was a form of bereavement: handing out mugs of hot tea and comfort to comrades of his lost son was a very real and positive memorial. All he had with him was a small stove, half a dozen enamel mugs, a few packets of tea, tins of sugar and condensed milk.

Lance-Corporal Cecil Withers (7/East Surreys) remembered the freezing days of April 1917 when the water froze in his bottle. He was rescued by a lady in a Salvation Army hut who opened a tin of Carnation condensed milk and poured it into his mess tin mixed with hot water and Horlick's malted milk.

The Customers

Wet and dry canteens, buffets, clubs, brasseries, soup kitchens and coffee stalls all tried to respond to what Tommies wanted, especially with items that French and Flemish establishments did not have for sale. Billy Nevill, at the time he was trying to stop his family and friends from sending so many parcels, gave as one of his reasons the fact that the canteens were so well stocked and inexpensive. However, when he was not near a canteen he still asked for butter and milk (April 1916).

By early 1915 the canteens had learnt that the staple diet preferred by Tommy behind the lines, and what he was going to *estaminets* and the like to enjoy, was egg and chips. He looked for the best and cheapest in this line. He would walk a long way to get it: Alfred Burrage and his chum, Dave Barney, walked three miles to a Salvation Army hut which had received rave reviews about its fare. Imagine their disappointment to arrive there and discover that it was closed for a prayer meeting. Frank Dunham also walked for miles to get to Ruyaulcourt (26 January 1918) for a bath, but the double attraction was the EF canteen there.

On pay of a shilling a day or a little more Tommy, especially if he was married and sending money home to his wife (more than unmarried men sent to their families), struggled to afford a daily plate of egg and chips and a little 'van blong'. Yet his chums usually rallied around him financially. A 'tarpaulin muster' was also possible where a group of Tommies threw in what money they had and everybody got an equal share. You needed very trustworthy mates to do this sort of thing.

Service

The service that the volunteers offered in the various canteens and huts was often exemplary, as you can see from the examples already shown.

1 Eating cold food. Cameron Highlanders at Contalmaison, September 1916.
(Reproduced by kind permission of the Imperial War Museum, Q.4133)

2 Lancashire Fusiliers being dished out with stew from a dixie, March 1917. (Reproduced by kind permission of the Imperial War Museum, Q.4843)

3 Cooking bacon over a brazier, near Ploegsteert Wood, March 1917. (Reproduced by kind permission of the Imperial War Museum, Q.4840)

4 A water cart comes to grief, St Eloi, 11 August 1917. (Reproduced by kind permission of the Imperial War Museum, Q.5942)

5 Parcels arrive, near Aveluy, September 1916. (Reproduced by kind permission of the Imperial War Museum, Q.1152)

6 Chinese labourers unloading 100-pound sacks of oats, Boulogne, 12 August 1917. (Reproduced by kind permission of the Imperial War Museum, Q.2700)

the fighting on the Western front. the outcome of this discussion was almost a disaster that evening. a member of the group riding in the lorry formed the impression that what he had been listening too was actually on the agenda for the following next day, of course for a long time now air activity had greatly increased and the rank and file had to be increasingly cautious at night respecting fire and naked lights. our evening meal was no different to what we usually received consisting of a portion of alleged Beef two potatoes boiled in the jackets, some rice and raisins, and probably one pint of tea with the allotted ration of rum added. later the Orderly officer called at each tent with two of the cooking staff to serve the pudding it was not so much pudding as conserve because it couldn't be sliced it was dished out with the aid of a spoon. after this repast there was a faint sign of merriment in the air. we were all rather pleased that no actual work was to take place outside the camp tomorrow. and that the call for cookhouse was to be at eight o'clock. a little later the fellow who had the Idea in his mind. that hostilities had ceased for the time being decided that the fire in his 'Tent' was in need of brightening up it happen'd to be an old bucket with hot coals, putting a cloth around the handle he carried the pail outside and commenced to whirl it around in a circle in a few seconds it was burning brightly, and he turned to return it to its position in the the tent just as aircraft warning whistles were

7 An extract from my father's diary about his less-than-solid Christmas pudding in 1917.

8 Rum leak? (Reproduced by kind permission of the Imperial War Museum, Q. 4619)

9 Unloading in Calais, 1917. (Reproduced by kind permission of the Imperial War Museum, Q.4809)

10 Bully beef.

11 Maconochie.

12 The Army Bakery in Calais, March 1917. (Reproduced by kind permission of the Imperial War Museum, Q.4793)

13 Sharing out the bread behind the lines near Ypres, August 1917. (Reproduced by kind permission of the Imperial War Museum, Q.5849)

14 Field kitchen, River Ancre area, October 1916. (Reproduced by kind permission of the Imperial War Museum, Q.1582)

15 Carrying insulated boxes, near Arras, March 1917. (Reproduced by kind permission of the Imperial War Museum, Q.4835)

16 How many to a bun? Near Arras, March 1917. (Reproduced by kind permission of the Imperial War Museum, Q.4846)

17 Cooking in a dixie lid on a 'home-made' brazier, May 1918. (Reproduced by kind permission of the Imperial War Museum, Q.583)

18 Two teams of British soldiers ploughing, near Arras, April 1918. (Reproduced by kind permission of the Imperial War Museum, Q.440)

19 Decauville light railway being constructed by the Royal Engineers near Querrieu, November 1916. (Reproduced by kind permission of the Imperial War Museum, Q.4614)

20 Soldiers at a coffee stall near Ovillers, late 1916. (Reproduced by kind permission of the Imperial War Museum, Q.1452)

21 Cooking on a scrounged stove, near Ovillers, July 1916. (Reproduced by kind permission of the Imperial War Museum, Q.3993)

22 The 2/RWF on the retreat from Le Cateau. Breakfast at Pointoise, 29 August 1914. (From the collection of Major–General R.C. Money)

23 A ration party of the 6/Queen's carrying 'hay boxes' along a communication trench near Arras, March 1917. (Reproduced by kind permission of the Imperial War Museum, Q. 4839)

24 Cooking in the lid of a mess tin, near Beaumont Hamel, 1916. (Reproduced by kind permission of Frontline Books)

25 My father, Private George Weeks, 24/Queen's. In Cologne, 1919.

TANTE'S COTTAGE –
BERLES AU BOIS. SEPT. 1915.

26 Tante's cottage at Berles-au-Bois, September 1915. (Drawing by Les Read)

27 A captured German field kitchen with its cooks, 1918. (Reproduced by kind permission of Leo Cooper)

28 Christmas dinner on the Somme, 1916. (Reproduced by kind permission of the Imperial War Museum, Q.1631)

'Sunny Jim' (otherwise Private Edge of the 2/RWF) worked in an EF canteen. The service he provided on 21 August 1916 was just a bit out of the ordinary. He walked seven miles to the trenches because he thought 'the boys' would like some more 'cigawettes'. He got to the trench, sold out and walked seven miles back.

Not every canteen was good. When the 1/8/Royal Warwickshires passed one outside Péronne on 26 April 1917 it was closed right in the middle of the day, but they managed to wake up a surly corporal in charge only to discover that he had no tea, coffee or cocoa. John Glubb described a coffee stall in the suburbs of Ypres (4 March 1916) as run by 'a clapped-out sergeant'. The next day a shell fell on it.

Rip-off

There were growing complaints about the prices charged in canteens. Variation in prices from establishment to establishment was criticised as much as the level of them. In 1916 battalion canteens were charging thirty centimes for a packet of cheap cigarettes ('gaspers'), but EF canteens charged fifty centimes (half a franc – about five pence) and Church Army huts were asking for one franc (ten pence – nearly a day's pay for the lowest-paid Tommy). Since canteens were often set up in response to high prices charged by civilian establishments, the fact that some canteens also over-charged aroused a lot of discontent.

In general, prices rose steadily throughout the war. In the *BEF Times* for 8 September 1917, 'Lieutenant Samuel Pepys' complained about a penny rise in the price of a packet of Woodbines (about fifteen per cent) and two pence on a tin of sardines (probably a bit more than ten per cent). The price of whisky rose by twenty-five per cent between 1914 and 1918. In August 1916 a question was asked in Parliament about EFC prices.

Regimental and battalion canteens generally had goods slightly cheaper than EF canteens. This was mainly based on the five per cent discount given by the latter when selling on to the smaller canteens. They relied on this to make a little profit whilst keeping prices low. This meant, for instance, that the 2/RWF canteen only added half a penny on articles up to a franc, with remissions on the lower-priced ones, and one penny for prices over this. Slices of cake, a cup of coffee or cold drinks

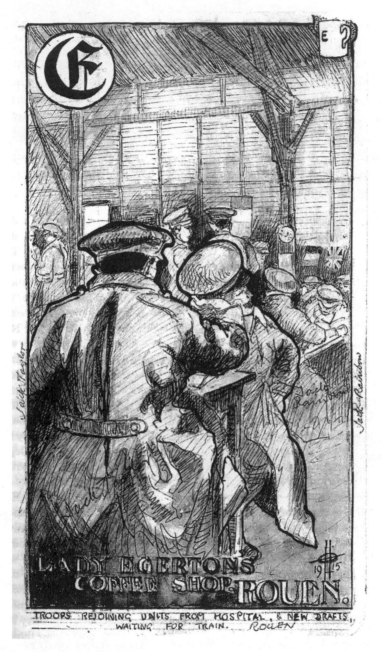

Lady Egerton's Coffee House in Rouen. Drawing by Henry Ogle.

were very profitable at a penny each. You could make five cups of tea for a penny, like Lyons's Corner House in the Strand.

This all came to an end at the beginning of 1918 when direct buying by the smaller canteens was banned; the 2/RWF's manager, a very entrepreneurial lance-corporal, had a father who ran a big business in England and bought a lot of supplies from him at reasonable prices. The new ruling meant that these canteens had to buy from the EF canteens and these promptly cancelled the five per cent discount. They had been losing business because of the lower prices elsewhere. The result was rising prices in all canteens in the last year of the war, making life even more difficult for cash-strapped Tommies.

What was Sold?

What was on offer in canteens? The answer was just about everything. Even the 2/RWF canteen in June 1916 had sixty items on sale including a wide range of sauces and meat and fish pies. Fags sold very well – except when a particular brand was issued in rations – but then sales of other types increased.

A YMCA marquee just behind the front near Albert in August 1916 had everything that could be eaten, mixed for drinking or smoked. There were sweet biscuits, slabs of cake, dates in fancy boxes, chocolates and sweets, oranges, tins of sweetened milk or cocoa, bottles of Camp coffee, Hoe's Sauce and tomato ketchup, and all types of tinned fruit – Bartlett pears being a big seller. It was all stacked on long trestle table counters. There were tins of sardines, herrings in tomato sauce, salmon and sausages. All brands of cigarettes were piled high. All Tommy needed was some money.

One could also purchase exotic items. Sergeant Walter Downing found lobster in a canteen in the light railway sidings at Bernafay (March 1918), and a brasserie at Ribecourt in 1918 offered an enormous range of cooked delicacies such as chicken and duck.

Disaster – 1918

It was during this month that the Germans launched their big offensive. The big canteens with their enormous stocks were in danger of being totally lost. A lot of the more expensive goods were sold off very quickly at a loss and troops made a good stab at removing the rest of it for free: some was left for the enemy, but not very much. A fortune was lost, in any case.

The 150 Brigade of the Royal Garrison Artillery sorted rapidly through the EFC in Bapaume, a very big one. Hundreds of boxes of fifty cigarettes were seized from the shelves. Gunners were photographed with cigars in their mouths and bottles of beer in hand, or vice-versa. One CSM carried away a case of café au lait, nine large tins of biscuits and five large packs of tobacco. The adjutant took 700 cigarettes, a roast chicken, two bottles of Grand Marnier and 144 boxes of Beecham's pills and an Ingersoll watch. Dinner in the RGA's mess that night was a grand occasion – prawns in aspic, cold boiled ham, pineapple with tinned cream, Pol Roger '86 and Johnny Walker whisky.

Near the Front

One of the amazing features of the smaller canteens was their proximity to the front line. A nonconformist minister gave up his post in England and worked in a YMCA canteen situated in an ex-German steel and concrete emplacement in Wytschaete just behind the Messines line. His cash box was a German machine-gun belt box. He had considerable trouble getting enough water but the CO of the Connaught Rangers (12 June 1917) let him know where there was a pile of petrol cans full of water that would not be missed.

Anyone could set up shop wherever they wished as long as they got permission from the British Army. They believed they were fulfilling a fundamental service by getting as near to the front line as possible, like Mr Hornung – who, incidentally, suffered from asthma and was grossly overweight. 'Wonderful people!' was Trooper George Jameson's (1/Northumberland Hussars) verdict on the Sally Army at Vimy, ready to serve tea at any hour of day or night and sometimes working under the most appalling conditions.

Lieutenant Ulrich Burke (2/Devons) said that if the Salvation Army or the Church Army could find a place where they could set up business, scrounge some wire netting and a piece of wood for a bed, there they would be, teapot in hand. One day it might be a Catholic padre running the show, the next a Protestant vicar, or a Jew or a Presbyterian.

They were always open for a drink and directions; this last service was very useful because men easily lost their way behind the front line (either coming or going) and this could be potentially dangerous. 'They were marvellous,' recalled Lieutenant Burke.

When Lance-Corporal Ernest Parker of the 10/Durham Light Infantry was in trenches near Arras in September 1916, a canteen was near enough to walk to and get a coffee, as long as he was quick and got back before 'stand to'. The YMCA canteen in the corner of Bazentin Wood near Albert was truly remarkable because it had so much stock so near the line. When the 1/8/Royal Warwickshires first spotted the marquee they thought it was a hallucination or a mirage. There it was – almost in the battlefield with its clean canvas, gleaming poles and guys and runners.

Frank Dunham, the stretcher-bearer, in December 1916 was on duty with a tunnelling company in case there were any accidents. Incredibly, they had a well-stocked canteen in a tunnel. It was probably in the safest place – unless German tunnellers discovered the tunnel and blew it up. So Frank fared well during this job, especially with cigarettes, chocolates and tinned fruit. He also recalled the battalion (1/19/Londons) canteen in Flesquières, right next to the front in February 1918. It was very near the EFC at Ytres and a Church Army tent, where the cocoa was excellent.

There were numerous coffee or cocoa stalls situated to give men a drink as they approached the line or left it. Frank Dunham frequented one just inside the Lille Gate in Ypres in November 1916. It served very hot cocoa out of old milk and fruit tins with the lids bent back to serve as handles. Crockery varied: Len Beechey (18/London Irish) was served coffee in a white glass with a spoon in a YMCA canteen. The little stall was in stark contrast to the rather grander casements under the city ramparts, offering a large range of alcoholic delights and a touch of night life.

Coffee stalls, however, were not universally popular. Dick Richards recounted how angry his fellow Fusiliers were when the rum ration was halved during the bitter weather of January 1917 and replaced by huts behind the line offering tea and a very small sweet biscuit.

Soup

Although what was on offer could vary enormously in quantity and quality, soup kitchens were also very welcome to weary soldiers. As the

5/Royal Warwickshires came out of the line in the Ypres Salient in October 1917 there was a stall offering good, thick soup in jam tins. George Coppard more or less stumbled across a soup kitchen near Givenchy on 6 December 1915 on his way to collect rations. This was serving 'shackles' – made from various ill-defined scraps. It was stirred enthusiastically with a large broom handle. Whatever was in it, two bowls made Coppard feel a lot warmer and nourished. Shackles probably inspired a piece in the *BEF Times* about 'Shavelings Soup Emporium', which employed a fully trained and qualified Soup Mixer. As a result of this enterprise Shavelings could guarantee that in future its wonderful soup would not contain more than seventy-five per cent coal dust but would have two per cent flavour.

Lieutenant Vaughan recalled something similar at Herbécourt on 14 March 1917. This concoction was billed as cabbage soup, a greasy liquid which just to look at made him feel sick. He didn't finish it; in fact, he didn't even start it.

Well-known Canteens

There were some very famous canteens, such as Lady Egerton's Coffee House in Rouen and Lady Angela Forbes's places at the base camp in Étaples. Lady Egerton's was a large, rather grim-looking hut, but inside it was painted in jolly colours and bedecked with the flags of all the Allied nations. The cocoa was a joy. It was a good place for a drink or a rendez-vous and a rest, somewhere perhaps to write your letter home.

Lady Angela Forbes's establishments provided relief for thousands of men enduring some very tough training routines in the 'Bullring', as the vast training grounds were called. It made a change from being hustled around by foul-mouthed NCOs, called 'Canaries'.

Talbot House in Poperinghe (remembered fondly as 'Pop' by Tommy) was an oasis of peace – although it was occasionally shelled – rest and good companionship. It was much more than a canteen and eventually spawned the 'Toc H' movement. You could get a decent meal and a (non-alcoholic) drink there. None of the religious or philanthropic organisations offered alcohol. You can gauge how popular it was by the fact that £11,000 profit was made in January 1918 alone. Its grocery section had 150 items for sale and was so successful that no EFC appeared to compete alongside it. There was a comfortable officers' club there in 1917 on the Ypres road opposite the station. Lieutenant Vaughan enjoyed an afternoon there on 29 July lounging in a deck chair and supping whisky.

Canteens of all types in Arras became essential by 1917 as all the civilian outlets had gone because of the proximity of the front line. By this time, too, Mr Hornung had opened several coffee stalls in the city. There was a wide variety of establishments in the base camps; Étaples had an EFC, YMCA huts and regimental institutes, apart from the other places already mentioned. The base camp at Harfleur had a wide range of Army canteens and YMCA and Salvation Army huts.

Battalion Canteens

Requests for extra Army canteens were often made by regiments or battalions if they felt there was a lack of outlets in any particular area. This was an urgent request if there was no English beer available in the vicinity. Billy Nevill's CO asked for a canteen in Ville-sur-Ancre in September 1915. When this was accepted Nevill became less reliant on parcels because of the excellent canteen provision of fresh fruit, tinned fruit, eggs and sweet biscuits.

EF canteens tended to be the best stocked, which was why the growing number of regimental and battalion canteens purchased a lot of their goods from them. By 1917 every regiment had a canteen. They were beginning to sell items not commonly available in EFCs, such as livestock, usually chickens. A few Tommies liked to maintain their own egg supplies.

The King's Own Yorkshire Light Infantry (dry) canteen was opened in April 1916 because there was no nearby EFC and, at least according to Lieutenant Spicer of the 9th Battalion, the French *estaminet* owners fleeced the troops. Another reason for starting up canteens was they helped to prevent food and drink being siphoned away from civilians, and also the competition tended to drive down prices in the *estaminets*.

One big problem not faced by EFCs was that regimental and battalion canteens had to follow their troops around as they changed division or their division moved. But the King's Own Yorkshire Light Infantry canteen was a great success, paying off its initial outlay within the first month and using a further surplus of 500 francs to augment rations for the regiment. The enthusiastic organisers then wanted to go for a wet canteen, potentially even more lucrative because there were so many complaints about weak beer and high prices in civilian places. However, they found it impossible to arrange a regular supply of decent beer despite contacting every brewery and beer depot within ten miles. Perhaps there were vested indigenous interests at stake here.

About the same time (spring 1916) the 2/RWF canteen got going. Within a month this had repaid start-up loans and still had left £16 worth of stock, £35 set aside for goods on order and about the same for an account to be opened at Cox's Bank. The canteen was expertly run by Lance-Corporal Mann, one of 'the old lot'. He was a very thorough manager, checking all the stock daily. Of course, there was always the chance of the whole lot being wiped out by a shell or break-ins from other old sweats. His father supplied tobacco, sweet biscuits, sausages, chocolate etc. at discount prices, and Mann sold these at shop prices. He was very upset when the CO refused to allow him to sell goods he got cheaply at new, increased prices.

Second Lieutenant Roland Ingle, preparing for the great battle to come (June 1916), left an account of a battalion 'canteen village', which had an officers' tea shop in addition to the normal grocery and hardware shops. Ingle was able to use the main canteen to supply the officers' mess with milk, fruit, bread, butter, coffee and tinned chicken (very expensive).

There were some divisional 'buffets', such as the one in the conservatory of a chateau at Ribement run by a mother and two daughters. Another one was run by two 'pretty and charming' sisters outside the divisional HQ at Heilly.

Twelve

Special Occasions

Christmas 1914

Most Tommies were able to celebrate Christmas in one culinary way or another, either behind the lines or in them. Many who couldn't had a later celebration. But 2nd Lieutenant Parsons spent Christmas Day 1914 in a haystack in the rain as a forward observation officer whilst his fellow officers ate roast goose in a French farm. In 1914 the 2/RWF had Maconochie for the first course but plum pudding for the second. Continuing good news was the arrival of two barrels of beer and a tray of nice glasses. The bad news was that the beer was French.

In the back areas Christmas sparkled because of the arrival of hordes of parcels from home. In 1914 the 1/Cameronians were in the village of Houplines when their stack of goodies arrived on 23 December, just right for the festive season.

Ordinary Seaman Myatt of the Royal Naval Division had a mixed Christmas Day, along with his pals. First they played a French unit at football (result not known), then lots of tobacco, cigarettes and plum puddings arrived, courtesy of funds run by national newspapers. But dinner was bully beef and hard biscuits and there was nothing alcoholic to drink. 'Never mind,' said the jolly Jack Tars and sang favourite ditties all evening.

The 2/Leicesters, coming out of the trench just in time for Christmas, after a surfeit of bully beef and biscuits (according to Private Frederick Dixon), came across a deserted farmhouse with pigs and chickens running about. Vegetables were ready in the garden, there was wine in the cellar and the 2/Leicesters were a very happy bunch. Seventy-five years later, Dixon reckoned he could still taste Christmas dinner 1914. However, there was a sad ending to this story because two of the Leicesters drank some methylated spirits and eventually died.

The 1/Hertfordshires, in a trench in the Ypres Salient, ate bully beef and a cold lump of Christmas pudding. But they did each get a Princess Mary gift box. Alfred Anderson of the 5/Black Watch also received one of these attractive boxes. The card in it read: 'With best wishes for a Happy Christmas and a Victorious New Year, from the Princess Mary and friends at home.' Anderson was a non-smoker and gave the tobacco and pipe and cigarettes away. But he kept the box and put the Bible his mother had given him in it. Another report claimed that the card read: 'From Mary and the women of the Empire.' One Tommy knew most of the ladies at the Empire Music Hall but he couldn't recall any 'Mary'.

Trying to cook a sizeable and varied meal in a trench dugout, usually no more than about six feet square, presented serious problems. Any cooking device had to share space with sundry soldiers trying to keep warm and sacks of fuel, tea and sugar. In the midst of it all, too, the enemy could be sending over 'iron rations'.

The 2/RWF celebrated Christmas on New Year's Day 1915 when they were at rest rather than attempt anything in the line. The officers had brandy-butter with the turkey, but the bread sauce came up with the plum pudding and the mess president was sacked, to be replaced by an officer who had worked in a London restaurant.

Christmas Truces 1914

Christmas 1914 was famous for its unofficial truces in many parts of the front. The Welsh Fusiliers were faced by Saxon troops, usually more amenable than Bavarians (at least at this stage of the war) and more likely to speak English having worked in England before hostilities. They kept shouting to the Fusiliers to come out, but the latter were reluctant to move because of a heavy ground fog and contented themselves with throwing out tins of bully beef and Tommy Tickler's and calling out, 'Here you are, you poor hungry bastards'. Eventually they did climb over the parapet and Captain Stockwell and a German officer met in No Man's Land, and the Saxons rolled over a couple of barrels of weak

French beer as a present. The Fusiliers gave them some plum pudding. An agreement was made not to fire until the next morning.

The 1/Royal Fusiliers also received beer and gave away cigarettes in return. They tried to start a football match with the Germans but a drunk German officer stopped his men from participating and the British played amongst themselves as the Germans watched. The 2/Argyll and Sutherland Highlanders also received barrels of beer and also two large bottles of lager and a box of very good cigars. The Scots presented them with some chocolates.

The Germans seemed well supplied with beer, both decent and French, something the Tommies rarely had in the trenches, and also cigars. The Queen's Westminster Rifles were presented with cigars in return for cigarettes. There is evidence that unofficial truces also took place before Christmas and afterwards. An account by Brigadier-General Heyworth about the Scots Guards at Mercur told of exchanges of cigars and whisky on 23 December and more on Boxing Day. The senior officers of Heyworth's division regarded the interlude as a good opportunity to have a rest and build or repair trenches.

Captain Sir Edward Hamilton Westrove Hulse, also a Scots Guard, recounted that he wanted the truce over late on Christmas Day but gifts were still being exchanged on Boxing Day afternoon. He presented German officers with Albany cigarettes and received cigars in return. Amazingly, officers from both sides joined in hunting hares in No Man's Land which had grown fat and slow on the cabbages growing there. George Paynter, a senior Scots officer, produced a very good bottle of rum, and that quickly disappeared.

Christmas 1915

For Christmas 1915 there were more special efforts than in 1914 to give the soldiers a festive day. There were some really grand menus. The 2nd Field Company, Royal Engineers, ate mince pies supplied by the CO's wife and there was a surfeit of tobacco. The following dinner was beautifully cooked:

Tomato Sauce
Sweetbread

Stuffed turkey with potatoes and peas
Plum pudding
Anchovies and sardines
Desserts
Coffee and port

This meal was served 800 yards from the German trenches and to prove it the diners heard the occasional shell or bullet coming over. The sappers were actually in grottos under Fonquevillers cemetery with a ventilation shaft. At the foot of the shaft the kitchen had been established with two ovens and two stoves taken from derelict houses. Not long after the meal was finished a German mine landed on the cemetery. The ground was already soaked with rain, with the result that fifty tons of earth and human remains fell on the kitchen. Luckily, by that time, the cooks were elsewhere.

Officers of the 2/RWF at Le Cornet Bourdois were in trouble in the days leading up to Christmas when they found that all the turkeys within a twenty-mile radius had already been snapped up. However, the cooks did them proud: Hors d'oeuvres, Consommé à la Royal, Rognons Saints, Dinde Rôtie, Pudding Noel, Sardines in Papier, Orange, Noix, Café – an early example of franglais.

This was only in one of the battalion's officers' messes: there were eleven in all and the CO and the adjutant felt obliged to visit all of them during the festive day and take a drink with them. This resulted in them downing five ports, three whiskies (of the 'barbed wire' blend) and a rum, claret and champagne, all the drinks in large glasses – tumbler, mug or mess tin. Miraculously, they managed to cross a plank over a ditch without falling in it. Unfortunately, however, they could not subsequently face their own Christmas dinners but only managed to 'leer' at some mince pies before collapsing into their beds.

There was a near disaster at 'A' Company where some villains stole the dixies containing the Christmas dinner. The cooks did a sterling job in retrieving it all, none the worse for wear. Then, an unexpected treat arrived from England just in time: plum pudding from one of the comforts committees.

There were some reports of unofficial truces on a much smaller scale than in 1914. Second Lieutenant Blacker of the 4/Coldstream Guards remembered an exchange of cigarettes in the Loos sector (photographs of the event were taken). Sergeant Read (17/Leicesters) described some fraternisation at Berles-au-Bois and gifts of cigarettes and cigars. It was then that the Leicesters realised that German 'water bottles' contained coffee and Schnapps.

Christmas 1916

The CO and the adjutant of the 1/King's Royal Rifle Corps had a similar experience on Christmas Day 1916 to their counterparts in the 2/RWF in 1915, when they had to call into no fewer than twelve messes and had twelve 'glasses' of port each. The battalion's war diary for that day was signed by the assistant adjutant. The 2nd Field Company, Royal Engineers, again fared well. There was a gift of turkeys from the CO, plum pudding from a fund in England and much extra fruit and vegetables; plus a metal gift cigarette case for everyone and a total of 52,000 Woodbines were distributed along with sacks of tobacco. It was all arranged by the father of the CO. The 2/Cameronians, in reserve, also did well for plum pudding. In addition, Captain Jack presented thirty-seven boxes of chocolate for fellow officers to send home to their families or friends.

Plum pudding – in those days a very traditional way of celebrating Christmas – was in abundance: each man in Billy Nevill's battalion of the East Surreys had to face two each. Even men who had little else got some pudding – Corporal James Brown Gingell, a sapper, ate only ration food but there was pudding to follow.

The 6/Cameronians had to wait until 2 January 1917 for their Christmas dinner, but perhaps the haggis specially made in Edinburgh for them more than compensated for this delay. They also had plenty to drink and Lance-Corporal John Jackson reported that he was the only man in the battalion who was not drunk.

There were still some rotten experiences. George Coppard (2/Royal Queen's West Surreys) had no parcels and only short and soggy rations handed out from a sandbag. There were a few raisins in them, covered in wet hairs. Llewellyn Wynn Griffiths, a Welsh Fusilier, suffered in a similar way but he did get some bad champagne. The 1/Cameronians, in huts at Bazentin-le-Petit, had no special food at all, not even as much as British Red Cross plum pudding. Moreover, they had to return to the trenches in the evening.

Nevertheless, there were some glorious feasts. The one experienced by the 18/King's Royal Rifle Corps was described by Captain Harry Yoxall as:

Tomato Soup
Curried prawns
Roast turkey and sausages, roast and mashed potatoes
Christmas pudding, minced pies, Devonshire creams, rum butter
Scotch woodcock on toast
Cheeses, caviare, apples, oranges, tangerines, almonds and raisins
Candied fruits, chocolate
Coffee
Veuve Cliquot 1906
Whisky, rum, port
Liqueur brandy 1891
Rum punch

They also had Christmas crackers!

The 2/RWF again did well although comforts committees only sent half a pound of plum pudding per man, but a similar amount also arrived from a private donor. The officers also had Christmas tea at 5pm as well as the earlier roast; there was cake, candied fruits and sweets, Veuve Cliquot and Benedictine.

The 17/Leicesters had to open a virtual avalanche of parcels. A Harrods hamper from the sister of one man – who was a buyer at Marshall and Snelgrove's – contained enough preserved ginger and Turkish Delight to stock a shop. Another package from the Army and Navy Stores was full of delicacies such as tongue, all beautifully wrapped. No one touched any of the ration food.

Once again there were veritable feasts in trying conditions. At Dranoutre near Messines the Connaught Rangers had no tables, chairs, plates or extra cutlery. The turkey was torn into shreds and served up in mess tins mixed with plum pudding. When these were emptied they were filled again with beer (hopefully, English beer). Winston Groom of the London Rifle Brigade remembered some hot rum punch. Private Cecil Withers (7/East Surreys) received the 'Daily Mail Christmas Pudding' in a two-pound flat, round tin. It didn't have a pip or a stork in it. 'Wonderful!' wrote Withers. Private Daniel Sweeney (2/Lincolns) saved his cake from a parcel until 4.30pm on Christmas Day in a trench. A 'blow-out' was the way he described it.

Frank Dunham waited till New Year's Day for his share of some pork. The QM of the 25/Londons bought a pig for each company from funds provided by the officers. The cooks improvised bigger ovens for the occasion. Christmas Day for Dunham was a mixture of poor rations and a few festive additions. A parcel provided some potted meat, smoked salmon, mince pies and other pastries, nuts and raisins. All this made the bully beef go down a bit more easily.

The 2/RWF celebrated on New Year's Day 1917. At HQ there was haggis (for a Welsh battalion!) for lunch and the 'southerners' loved it. At the YMCA Mrs 'Tiger' Phillips and a friend came to dinner and managed:

Vermouth
Hors d'oevres
Clear Soup
Sole and perfect sauce
Roast Turkey and sausage
Celery
Plum pudding
Savoury (enigmatic but delicious)
Veuve Cliquot
Port
Benedictine
Coffee

Christmas 1917

Christmas 1917, for Rifleman B.F. Eccles (7/The Rifle Brigade), meant four days in a hole on Passchendaele Ridge, but he did get a belated Christmas dinner at St Omer, along with cigarettes and a good pipe. Len Beechey (18/London Irish) got five dates but a few days later someone gave him a mince pie and a piece of plum pudding. Alfred Burrage of the Artists' Rifles – in the trenches in bitterly cold weather near Cambrai – did get some real butter and a small portion of Christmas pudding and an extra dollop of jam. Otherwise it was

The well at Fonquevillers. Drawing by Henry Ogle.

bully beef and a quarter of a loaf, although a bloke with a parcel shared round some nuts.

In stark contrast, NCOs and men of the 1/1/South Midlands Field Ambulance had roast pork and 'all the trimmings', plum pudding, apples, oranges, wine and cigarettes. The printed menu announced that the chef was Lance-Corporal Draycott and his assistants were Privates Hood and Raybould.

My father's officers brought round some 'alleged beef' and some pudding which was so watery he drank it rather than ate it. Happily, a nearby artillery battery sent over some strong ale with bits of pudding floating around in it. On Boxing Day he got an orange, a few dates and chestnuts. There was no hot food that day because a bomb dropped by a plane fell on the camp on Christmas night and all the cooks got Blighty Ones.

Officers of the 13/Royal Fusiliers were quite pleased with their Christmas, however. They travelled into Locre and had a hot bath in a nunnery followed by hot Malaga (sweet raisin wine) in a nearby *estaminet*. Officers of the 2/RWF paid a subscription each of £7 in order to purchase a turkey at three shillings and two pence a pound – the whole bird costing thirty shillings, half a week's pay for an officer. The 2/RWF were in Poperinghe. Everybody got something special. The signallers and runners had cocktails of beer and champagne, and each officers' mess had its own show as usual. One menu was:

Hors d'ouvre
Clear oxtail soup
Fresh whiting
Dressed cutlet in celery
Stuffed turkey and trimmings
Plum pudding (made by the cook)
Angels on horseback
Dessert
Apples, oranges, dates, walnuts
Veuve Cliquot
Kummel
Coffee

Other Celebrations

There were other dates in the year to celebrate. Welsh regiments observed St David's Day – 1 March. The 2/RWF officers held their dinner in 1916 in Béthune and one officer was reported to have crawled a quarter of a mile back to his billet. On 1 March 1918 a serious lack of plates, glasses and cutlery was solved by the generosity of local *estaminets*, resulting in the following:

Consommé of Gallos
Merlin Duglers
Escallops de Vènu Vilanaires
Gigot de Monton Rote
Pommes rissoles, chous bruxelles
Pudding au Chocolate
Scotch woodcock
Dessert
Café
Veuve Cliquot
Benedictine
Kummel
At gris pot

Unfortunately, there was no port from the Portuguese canteen, who said they didn't have any – a likely story!

The Old Etonians Day was 4 June. In 1917 300 Old Etonians sat in order of seniority according to the dates they were in the school. The 8/East Surreys also commemorated the anniversary of their formation on 10 September 1915. They washed down chicken de l'arc, Noé and Péche in tins with a red wine called 'Graves'. For the regimental mess night of the King's Own Yorkshire Light Infantry in May 1917 a complete dinner service for forty was hired from Amiens.

Resting in Airaines in July 1917 the 2/RWF organised a Gala Day on the 22nd, inviting all the citizens of the town to tea. However, the battalion made a serious financial loss on the beer tent. This had to be sited out of the way in deference to the divisional general's dislike of alcohol. Because of very poor sales the battalion had to compensate the brewery, to the tune of 800 francs. Another 2,000 francs was lost due to the misdirection of consignments of beer to the 1st Battalion (which said, 'Thank you very much') and the 8th Battalion, which was in Mesopotamia. The battalion also commemorated their 'tour' in the front line ending in July 1917. On the 8th there was a fine dinner in Airaines at seventeen francs a head:

Hors d'oevres
Soup
Sole
Cutlet Reforme
Roast chicken etc.
Strawberries
Angels on horseback
Whisky and Perrier
Veuve Cliquot
Port
Cognac
Coffee

There were also concerts, birthday parties, sports days and countless football matches, all noted for a conspicuous consumption of food and drink, notably beer, although champagne was the order of the day (officers only) at the concert organised by John Glubb for the 7th Field Company of the Royal Engineers. The 1/Hull Pals thoroughly enjoyed Private Clappison's glorious birthday party on 22 September 1918, to which even the HQ were invited. It was reported that Private Clappison was 'all but drunk'.

18 June 1917 saw the annual sports day of E Corps Signal Company, with an EFC providing refreshments. The 1/8/Royal Warwickshires also held a successful sports day on 25 July 1917, following which the CO gave out cash prizes to all the winners. These were spent to the last penny on 'wet' refreshments of one sort or another, to the extent that Corporal McKay, returning to his billet in triumph, lay down his oilsheet on the muddy floor of a barn and promptly went to sleep beside it.

At the 8/East Surreys inter-company football competition on 10 September 1915, the traditional half-time lemon was unavailable and was replaced by a sandbag of apples. There were also no lemons at the 1/19/Londons Shrove Tuesday occasion on 13 February 1918, or for that matter any pancakes, but some popular rissoles were on offer.

Thirteen

On the Move – Retreats and Advances

Scale of the Movements

To give some idea of the scales of the retreats and advances of 1914 and 1918, in contrast to the relatively static warfare of 1915–17, approximate distances are given here. The British retreat from Mons in Belgium to Le Cateau in France between 24–26 August 1914 covered about forty miles. Further retreat between 26 August and 1 September from Le Cateau to the River Marne near Paris measured about sixty miles. The French counter-attack from the Marne drove the Germans back thirty miles to the River Aisne by 8 September. Following this campaign the rest of September was spent by both sides moving north towards the sea in Flanders and establishing the most advantageous front lines. It is about eighty miles from the River Aisne to Ypres. Compared to trench warfare this was very extensive and rapid movement.

The German offensive beginning on 21 March 1918 reached Péronne on the 23rd, an advance of fifteen miles. By the 28th Albert had fallen. April saw attacks south of the Ypres Salient which achieved an advance of fifteen miles beyond Armentières within a few days.

Back to the south the Germans arrived near Amiens by 24 April, almost forty miles from the line of 21 March. Advances even further south against the French reached the River Marne from the Aisne (thirty miles) on 1 June, a reverse of the September 1914 battle. By that time, however, the Germans were running low on steam.

In July 1918 Allied counter-attacks began to take effect and included the new US Army, which launched its first successful offensive in

September. Between then and the Armistice (11 November) the British moved from Passchendaele to near Ghent (forty miles), from Arras to Mons (fifty miles) and from Albert to near Charleroi (sixty miles).

Logistics

The logistics of getting supplies to a quickly retreating Army presented a whole host of problems. In August 1914 the lines of supply were only beginning to take shape. Trying to feed troops whose whereabouts were uncertain in a territory new to the British Army was well-nigh impossible. Then the retreat quickly reversed gear, stretching the new supply lines. Liaising with the railway staff of a foreign country and getting used to its roads was a very difficult task, but not as bad as when retreating. Keeping behind an advancing Army was much easier than falling back with a retreating one.

By 1918 there was an established and complex system of supply, but even this was thrown into chaos in March and April by the unexpected rapid retreat of the British. But by May the brunt of the attacks was being borne by the French and further north supply lines began to return to normal. A further three to four months elapsed before supply lines had to stretch again, giving command more time to plan for this, and there was nothing like the disruption of a few months earlier, or the problems of advancing experienced in 1914. One big difference was the victorious Army of 1918 was generally supplied daily with hot food. Experiments with air drops of supplies were tried out.

Retreat from Mons – 1914

The bulk of the Old Contemptibles was half-starved on the retreat from Mons in August 1914. The 1/Cameronians marched eighteen miles in a day with only one cold meal. The retreating Army was a rabble of mixed units. Individuals and small groups attached themselves to any others who had some food or appeared to know where some might be found. It took the Cameronians two and a half days of ceaseless marching to get to Le Cateau, eating only a few scraps.

Traffic chaos on the roads meant that little food got through. 120 Battery, Royal Artillery, stumbled back with the infantry, trying not to abandon all their big guns. Between Mons and St Ghislain local citizens offered them food but the gunners felt too sick and downhearted to accept, and officers ordered them not to take wine or beer, or even water in case it was poisoned or drugged. The 4/Middlesex was also offered food and drink by villagers in Mesvin – biscuits, chocolate, water, fruit and bread, but they ate little because they were only allowed a short rest in a corn field in order to keep up the momentum of the retreat from the hotly pursuing Germans.

Frustrated by their inability to deliver food to specific units, transport tended to leave dumps of it in fields or by the side of roads hoping that some men would find it. The 2/RWF, coming across such a dump, also had little time to take advantage of it except to cram some hard biscuits into their haversacks. They even scrounged a meal from some gypsies. Some fleeing civilians were even hungrier than the soldiers and the Fusiliers shared what was left of their emergency rations with them.

Gunner J.W. Palmer of the Royal Field Artillery went some days without food and just a little water, just enough to keep him alive. It was a precarious existence because their guns were pulled by horses who suffered greatly from the lack of food and water. The gunners were more concerned for their horses than themselves. They managed to get some corn from the fields for them. During this period of 24–26 August a pilot, Lieutenant W.R. Read, had no food after damaging his plane landing at Bertoy. He eventually got a lift in a staff car trying to crawl through the packed roads of men, vehicles and horses.

On 27 August, in St Quentin, the CO of the 2/RWF requisitioned a grocer's shop despite the owner's protests. The Fusiliers got potted meat, jam, sweet biscuits and chocolate. Some townspeople brought out a large jug of beer, more chocolate and some bread. But Major Williams ordered one man not to accept a bottle of wine – not because of poison but of possible inebriation. This Tommy whispered to a pal that he'd need ten bottles of the stuff to get sozzled. By this time the battalion had marched thirty-three miles with very few stops.

Cooks were having a hell of a time trying to move their mobile kitchens, sometimes across muddy fields to avoid the crammed roads. Horses found it difficult to pull the limbers over rough country, often uphill. Even if the cooks arrived at the rendezvous with their respective units they might not have enough water, because the water tankers were finding it very difficult to get past traffic moving in the opposite direction.

At Pontoise on 28 August, after another sixteen miles, the Welsh Fusiliers' QM had organised stew, tea and an issue of rum. The 1/Cameronians were there at the same time and Captain R.H.W. Rose didn't relish the scum on the top of the stew, but he consumed his portion nonetheless because he was starving. Valenciennes looked more likely to provide more and better food on the next day, with mobile kitchens ready and cooking, but the Germans got there very quickly and the cooks beat a hasty retreat.

The roads south of Valenciennes were lined with apple and pear trees and the ripe fruit made a nice change from bully beef, hard biscuits and 'mousetrap' (mouldy cheese). A rabbit also found its way into a dixie of stew. Arthur Osburn, the MO of the 4/Irish Dragoons Guards, remembered the scents of clementines and wild blackberries near Le Cateau.

The 1/Cameronians were actually issued with rations on 29 August and their cooks produced hot meals and there was time for a smoke, a chat and some sleep. French citizens also provided pails of water, some wine and long rolls of buttered bread and some fruit. They gave whatever they had. After walking forty-four miles from Le Cateau without a proper meal for thirty-six hours, this was bliss.

Despite the fact that fortunes had changed on the battlefield by 1 September, supplying food was still difficult in the Marne area. The 2/Scots Guards were lucky enough to find a deserted grocer's shop in Meaux on 2 September and helped themselves to boxes of biscuits and tins of sardines.

September Advances – Rations Getting Through

By 4 September the 2/RWF were getting rations every day, mainly because at the food dumps the QM answered 'yes' to the name of any battalion. Captain Rose of the 1/Cameronians, crossing the Aisne on 15 September, reported that the rations for the battalion were good. The crisis appeared to be over. The Old Contemptibles were ready to accept that it had been difficult to feed them, but now any deficiencies were met with complaint, particularly the lack of cigarettes. Only a few packets of 'Caporal' were handed out, no substitute for Woodbines.

By 8 September the Welsh Fusiliers were eating very well. Officers of 'A' Company had a comparatively sumptuous meal in a chateau. Even the burgundy, which had been hidden in a haystack by the owner, was respectable and the officers became 'animated'. About this time Private Dick Richards and his pals ate the remains of a very good dinner left by the retreating Germans in a house – roast chicken, duck, vegetables and bottles of wine. The worry was that it had been poisoned, but Dick and his mates were very hungry and took a chance.

Supply to specific battalions became more and more organised throughout September as the BEF moved north towards Ypres. Meals became regular: the 1/Cameronians at Septmonts on the Aisne in early October were getting a cup of soup with bread or biscuits at 9pm every night. French citizens were also still handing out food and drink – perhaps their most generous period of the war. The Welsh Fusiliers were given chocolate and bread by people in Bailleul on 7 October.

First Battle of Ypres

Not all battalions would fare so well as they settled into the early trenches of the Ypres Salient. The First Battle of Ypres was a bitterly fought struggle, with the Germans threatening to break through on several occasions. Private Clifford of the 1/Hertfordshires remembered a period of two to three weeks when he had no proper meals and no hot food at all. Trooper George Jameson, 1/Northumberland Hussars, described rations in these days as 'very chancy'. On 31 October he and other cavalrymen were delighted to find some champagne in a cellar in Gheluvelt. They had no time to sample any, however, so they strapped four bottles each to their saddles and rode off hurriedly. Sadly, the movement caused the corks to pop off and only the horses were showered with champagne.

Retreat 1918

In 1918 the flying retreat of March and April revived the scenes of August 1914, only on a much larger scale, both in terms of area and also the number of British troops involved. Again it became a matter of finding whatever food you could as ration supplies disintegrated. Lieutenant Ulrich Burke (2/Devons) recalled that he never knew when he would pick up any grub.

Tens of thousands of civilians were also caught up in the chaos, displaced from their homes as they had no intention of coming under the jurisdiction of the enemy – tales from places like Lille convinced them that it was better to leave their homes than allow the tide of war to engulf them.

Soldiers searched desperately for food in their pell-mell flight. Men of the 9/Royal Sussex found a farm and killed and cooked a calf and ate lumps of it, killed chickens and took every scrap of food they could find, even grains of rice from a drawer. They frenziedly grabbed as many as they could of the black bottles in a cellar, probably containing cider: they didn't waste time trying to find out what it was. There was no time to lose before moving again quickly.

In Corbie near the Somme the citizens had fled so suddenly that bread was left cooking in ovens and soup was bubbling in pots; this kept Sergeant Walter Downing going. His next meal was cold stew and tepid cocoa on Hill 104 two days later and he wolfed it down. Similarly, the 2/7/Worcesters ate a dinner still cooking in the kitchens of an abandoned hospital in Méricourt. They ate that and cleared out the stocks of whole cheeses, boxes of dates, sweet biscuits, meat and tins of many types of meat, fish and fruit.

377 Battery, Royal Artillery, running their big guns through the village of Flavy, had no time to take advantage of the many chickens, ducks, an old sow and her piglets that they found there. The battery fired at the enemy all night, but the Germans came pouring over a canal and the gunners had to beat a very hasty retreat, butchering the sow and taking the carcass with them. Yet in the next few days they found no time to prepare and cook it and eventually threw it away.

On 21–22 March the Germans advanced fifteen miles, firing three million shells. Frank Dunham – by then an aid post orderly – got no rations and was saved by a parcel he had received from home. Alfred Burrage of the Artists' Rifles thought his luck was in with the two EF canteens in Ytres, but every scrap of stuff had been removed except a few packets of cigarettes and some Epsom Salts. He took a chance drinking some greenish-looking water, possibly harbouring mustard gas. Dunham had arrived in Ytres earlier that day to witness the actual looting of the canteens – men trampling wildly over stacks of upturned boxes, littered tins and packets. The aid post MO ordered him not to wait but to maintain contact with the battalion in the race to escape the enemy.

Dunham was in Rocquigny on 23 March, when the order of the day was 'no smoking' in case their presence in the village alerted the German artillery. One man totally ignored the order, desperate for a fag, and others began to do the same. On 24 March limbers arrived with a few rations. Company cookers were due to arrive but they didn't show up all day and hopes of hot stew and a drink faded and finally expired.

The headlong retreat severely disrupted nascent agricultural enterprises by the Army. Special new farms had to be abandoned on 24 March and the machinery and equipment was taken back to Rouen. Troops who had looked forward to driving tractors were sent back into the front line to fire rifles instead.

As well as numerous EF canteens, seven YMCA huts and five Church Army huts lost all their stores, but plundering by German troops tended to slow up their advance and must have contributed to their gradual loss of momentum. Another effect of the offensive was that the surviving EF canteens (even in areas well away from the Somme) rushed food in lorries right up to divisional transport lines to sell at inflated prices – sweet biscuits at 6.15 francs a packet (normal price: 4.75 francs) – far beyond the pocket of the ordinary Tommy.

On 26 March Private Burrage was on the run and starving. He found a bottle of red wine, drunk the lot and became inebriated in the cellar of a town house, surrounded by dead victims of shelling. A padre found him there and gave him a tin of sardines. A villager later refused him some eggs on the grounds that the British Army was cowardly because it was running away from the Germans, and anyway, the Australians had cut his chickens' throats. Another villager did offer him a chicken as long as Burrage or one of the other men with him wrung its neck. But none of them could do it. On the 27th Bombardier Dudley Gyngell seized twelve tins of sardines from an EF canteen and also considered taking the piano, but abandoned the idea as impractical.

Frank Dunham was in a support trench near Serlis on 28 March; there was plenty of farm food there – chickens, eggs and vegetables. There was very little bread so Frank boiled hard biscuits into a hash and mixed it with jam. He collected a store of apples in a cellar in Bazincourt on 7 April and

An Army limber. Drawing by Henry Ogle.

some potatoes in another one and tins of jam from a third. The aid post cook found an oven and cooked the lot into a nutritious hash.

Burrage reached the Ancre by the same day and the Australians cooked him some rissoles but stole his rum. Meeting up with your unit's cooks was a difficult business. The 1/Hull Pals managed to encounter theirs in Pommier to get their first hot meal in days. On the same day the Connaught Rangers met a very distressed lady in Bray on the Somme who was having to leave behind 100,000 francs' worth of property. The CO promised to post sentries to guard her belongings. In her gratitude she presented him with three pigs, but the Rangers never had a chance to eat them before being hurriedly moved off towards Amiens. After they left Bray they had no meal for thirty hours until an artillery battery gave them some food. The CO, Major Rowland Fielding, got some chocolates, a bag of biscuits and some port, all of which he scoffed down ravenously.

The 2/RWF were in Doullens at this time getting handouts of cigarettes, chocolates and sweet biscuits from the EF canteen there. A café in the town charged an exorbitant price (three francs) for some tepid tea, a mouthful of omelette and a scrap of bread. They got to Bazincourt where they fared better because all the civilians had fled and there were hens and pigeons fluttering about.

The artillery was also having a rough time trying to ward off the Germans, saving their guns and trying to find something to eat at the same time. The officers of 377 Battery were so stressed that some of them, starving, went on a desperate diversion into Crisolles. Lieutenant Smith, finding half a bottle of wine, gulped it down on an empty stomach, collapsed into an easy chair and fell into a deep sleep. The enemy was very near so his comrades poured a bucket of water over him and dragged him off, half-conscious.

The 1/Cameronians – retreating past Beuvry on 8–10 April – had no food except emergency hard biscuits. On the 10th they were called into the front line because a Portuguese battalion had fled. The Cameronians were in Estars the following day and shared out a huge barrel of wine. Lance-Corporal John Jackson found chickens and eggs. There was also a pig, which met a soldier's death after several attempts by amateur butchers. The resulting pork was very much enjoyed by the battalion. Also, in the cellar of almost every house was wine, beer and stout. But, once again, time for consumption was all too brief to make serious inroads into it. Battalion police were left to destroy all of it and deny the enemy a drink or two. However, some of the 'old soldiers' managed to hide some of the stout in 'empty' boxes and return for it just as they were leaving.

The Cameronians continued their flight towards Béthune and again had very little to eat between 15–20 April. It was not really until May that the German push towards Amiens lost its momentum and some battalions were able to eat proper rations again. Even throughout June, however, some units were struggling to get reasonable supplies. Lieutenant Blacker remembered being extremely thirsty and buying a pail of milk from a farmer in Bienville. The 2/Cameronians were only receiving snatches of food at the end of this month. Lieutenant Carr of 377 Battery met Field Marshal Haig in Abbéville around this time and reported to him that his men and horses had survived over ten days in June with little and sometimes no food.

Allied Offensive 1918

By early July the Allies were storming back into attack. Problems of supplying food to advancing troops re-emerged. They were moving into areas with no trench systems, having to shelter in shell holes whilst ration parties struggled up with food over open ground for half a mile or more. The capture of entrenched enemy positions, however, eased these early problems: some of them also contained food, sometimes still warm. Cecil Withers tasted samovars for the first time in his life along with some very tasty, hot coffee.

Between 30 September and 7 October 1918 the advance travelled across the battlefields of three Battles of Ypres, right across the Salient and beyond. To kick off this offensive eighty aircraft dropped 15,000 ration packs to forward troops. Next day, the well-fed Tommies captured the whole of the Third Ypres battlefield. The ghosts of hundreds of thousands of men must have sighed.

Food and drink could now be picked up from deserted houses and farmhouses. Second Lieutenant Read, returning as a newly promoted officer to the 8/Leicesters, harvested cabbages, potatoes, carrots and turnips near Wevelghem beyond the Salient. There was also oil for his stove and some nice crockery.

In the conditions of advance some Tommies tended to accumulate too much food – too much because they had to carry it, and at a rare pace by October. Sapper Arthur Halestrop, a Royal Engineer in the 46th Division supporting the attack on the Hindenburg Line, was humping about a six-day supply of bully beef and canned fruit, biscuits and bread in a sandbag. He got so fed up he threw it away, deciding to rely on what he could pick up from the fleeing Germans. It didn't work out that way, however, and he was finally left with some mud-encrusted biscuits which he had to wash in water from a petrol can. The discovery of a packet of oatmeal on a railway line kept him going for several days, despite the frustrating disadvantage of not being able to convert it into burgoo through lack of water.

The speed of the advance and the state of the German Army late in October is well illustrated by the case of Trooper Ben Clowting of the 4/Royal Irish Dragoon Guards. This battalion held a great number of prisoners on a farm. Clowting was told that a lot of them had actually been rounded up on the farm after killing the guard dog and eating it, along with lumps out of a dead horse. Clowting exchanged a three-quarter-pound tin of bully beef for a watch from a prisoner. Even then the German's luck was not in because Clowting had to throw the tin over a fence and it hit the wretched prisoner on the head.

Ration supply could still be uncertain in November. On the 8th, just three days before the Armistice, Private MacLean was eating wet bread, filthy cheese and drinking a little tea brewed over a candle.

'Victory'

Ecstatic, liberated civilians celebrated their release from four years of German occupation. Frank Dunham stocked up at an EF canteen in order to bring the family with whom he was billeted with in Lille the sort of food that they had not eaten all those years. On 29 October they cooked a superb meal from his gifts and served it on nice plates on their best white tablecloth, and it was eaten with silver cutlery which had been hidden away during the occupation. Buried wine was excavated from the garden.

Second Lieutenant Read liberated villagers (and their goats) from a stinking cellar in Knocke on 17 October. The civilians were extremely joyful and very emotional. They enthusiastically offered goats' milk, chips and rotten ersatz coffee. Great pans of chips were fried from the stack of potatoes they had kept with them in the cellar, and sent up in relays to the Tommies of the 8/Leicesters who had liberated them. In the freed village of Aeshoek the young children had either never seen chocolate or forgotten what it was. The 1/Hull Pals also recalled the generosity of the people of Wattieles, a suburb of Roubaix. They were plied with every scrap of food and drink the villagers possessed.

The news of the Armistice on the 11th had a rather strange effect on the soldiers. Corporal Clifford Lane (1/Hertfordshires) was too exhausted to show any kind of emotion. All he wanted to do was get back to his billet to sleep. He and his pals greeted the announcement with silence: no one wanted a celebratory drink. Even though the Honourable Artillery Company did have a drink, no one got even tipsy. Corporal Reginald Haine remembered realising that he could finally stand up straight without risking being shot at.

The officers of the Somerset Light Infantry arranged a dinner and drank their last bottles of whisky, but it was a strangely subdued occasion. Desmond King (King's Royal Rifle Corps) also felt no exhilaration as he ate a cold lunch. He did, however, notice two cooks with their arms around each other singing. Perhaps they should have been cooking King some hot food.

Guy Chapman said he felt 'very old, very tired and very wise'. He ate a meal listlessly: the food was listless, too. But the American MO, supposedly a teetotaller, appeared to be drunk and danced a caçhucha. Chapman gazed at him without enthusiasm and put him to bed.

In Mauberge the 377 Battery did do some celebrating when a villager dug up several bottles of cognac and also supplied some champagne. The officers of this largely Scottish unit, after polishing off all this booze, sang 'Scots Wha Hae' and seized the only Englishman amongst them and tried to pull off his trousers.

Fourteen

On the Move – Moving to and from the Trenches

On the March

Charles Carrington of the 1/5/Royal Warwickshires counted the number of times his battalion moved to and from the front in 1916. It was eighty times. Sixty-six of these movements were by foot, and fourteen by train or bus. Even then, they had to march, probably miles (it was fifteen miles to the railhead at Corbie from the front), to get on the train or the bus. From this analysis, it is apparent that the main method of troop mobility was on foot.

Long marches could be extremely hard going because of the amount of equipment and supplies Tommy had to carry. Elmer Wilfred Cotton listed a typical load in his 1915 'Notebook'. About his person, in addition to his clothes (which, in poorer weather, would include a very heavy greatcoat), Tommy had a field dressing, service pay book, identity disc and jack knife, two smoke helmets, a bottle of iodine and a waterproof sheet. Hanging from him was his mess tin, rifle and sling, oil bottle, a pull through, bayonet and scabbard. There was an excavating tool to hump along, and its carrier, a water bottle, a haversack packed with further belongings, and 250 rounds of ammunition. The haversack and a valise contained spare clothing, washing materials, a greatcoat (if he wasn't wearing it he had to carry it), a blanket, cutlery and iron rations. This load could weigh thirty-five kilos or more, a tremendous burden over as much as twenty miles a day. Private Tom MacDonald (9/Royal Sussex) said that he just fell down, totally whacked, with his load from where he stood when the order to stop came. He could even sleep whilst marching along.

Cold, wet or hot weather made life even harder. Men died of heat exhaustion on the march. Major Vignoles of the Grimsby Chums noted the bad language employed in these circumstances but he understood their constant frustrations. 'No harm, sir', they would add with a grin after a barrage of obscenities.

Marching to Rest Areas

At least marching away from the front, even to a support camp, was better than marching to it. Tommy sang on his way out but not on his way back to the line. If he was going to billets he could look forward to not being shot at or shelled or bombed (although as the war went on there was more chance of this behind the lines), a good rest and some nice egg and chips in an *estaminet*. As he trudged along he might pass soup kitchens, coffee stalls and even a canteen, and imagine he was returning to civilisation for a couple of weeks. Going towards the war was a different story.

The 2/West Yorkshires went back to Citadel Camp (Somme) in November 1916 and took three and a half hours to march five miles. When they arrived at the camp, transport and the field kitchens had not arrived, which was unusual. There was no food and hot drinks. After a short while the QM managed to borrow some food from another outfit – dixies of hot stew, a reviver, although a relatively poor example of this culinary art. It did contain kippers, however, on top of the meat, vegetables, biscuits, Maconochie and beans. The officers had to wait longer for their food because all the cooking pots, plates and cutlery used for them (they didn't carry them) were still with the missing transport. Even when this did arrive they only got cold bully beef, poorly heated Maconochie and rashers of fried ration beef.

It was not unusual on marches for officers to fare worse than their men. Charles Carrington made this observation with reference to the 1/5/Royal Warwickshires. In fact, most of the transports of the 2/West Yorkshires were held up for days before arriving at Citadel Camp and the QM had to scrounge for water and scraps for his fellow officers.

Stops en Route

Some rests en route to the billets or camps lasted long enough for Tommy to knock up some 'sergeant-major' tea, or perhaps the cooks would be allowed to get some dixies of stew and tea for them – accompanied by loud cheers. There might even be time for a greasy rasher of bacon or two, but generally food at stops consisted of biscuits and jam. Whatever it was they had to eat it pretty quickly before being ordered to their feet again.

The 17/Leicesters reached St Leger in April 1917 with heavy shells falling around them. The cooks got there before the infantry, and the Tommies could smell the hot soup and tea as they approached the stopping place. Soon grimy old soldiers (cooks tended to be a bit older) stood by the dixies, ladles in hand, with grinning, welcoming expressions lit up by the half-open doors of the fires.

Eric Gore-Brown (Post Office Rifles) recalled overnight stops when marching out of the line as pleasant occasions – memories of hot tea and dim figures in the breaking dawn with pipes and cigarettes like myriad glow-worms. There could be nice surprises on the march, such as roadside orchards full of apples or pears. Tommy was a great scrumper, proved by the 25/Londons as they raided an orchard near Anzin St Aubin on 26 October 1917.

Wet weather could make life distinctly unpleasant. The 2/RWF was moving to bivouacs at Bécondel on 30 August 1916 and had to march over ground saturated with rain; they were already on quarter rations because of transport difficulties. At each stop there was a long wait for the mess cart because the horses had been struggling badly trying to get the wagons over muddy hills.

The 17/Leicesters – stopping on their way out of the line while heading towards billets in St Sylvestre in 1915 – were without rations and so ate any scraps they had in their haversacks (Tommy was a great hoarder) or mess tins, left over from previous rations or parcels. Private Read gathered together some bread and cheese and some cakes from a parcel. At least there was tea.

Sometimes the marchers even went without tea when water supplies were scarce. In these circumstances, men could only drink from their quart water flask. Even then, they were rationed on the amount they could drink on hot days in order to make it last until they reached their destination.

On 22 July 1915 Private John Jackson of the 6/Cameronians drank all his water against orders and tried to catch rain drops in his mess tin.

Going Back to the Trenches – Hard Times

All these troubles could also accompany Tommy on his way to the trenches, and there was not a lot to look forward to when he got there. It was even worse if it was his first time at the front. At least if rations kept up the soldiers could eat quite well. The 17/Leicesters actually had tins of superior American pork and beans going into the line south of Ypres at Wulverghem in 1915. There was no such luck for the Royal Horse Artillery in March 1916, slogging their way through freezing weather for fourteen miles in a day towards Arras, with no food for twenty-four hours. They marched the next two days too, including another spell of fifteen hours without rations. When the rations did arrive they were short.

The 2/RWF marched for twelve days north towards Arras and the battlefield in April 1917 in freezing conditions. They set off on the 2nd and arrived on the 14th in front of the Hindenburg Line at St Martin Cojuel. On some of these days, especially the 12th, food was in very short supply. On arrival late at night they didn't get a hot drink until the following morning, and it was snowing as well. A lot of the men were suffering from constipation or diarrhoea because of poor and inadequate food and the hardships of the march. Others pretended to suffer from one of these conditions. Ailing Tommies could fall by the wayside hoping to finish up on one of the wagons. It was difficult for officers to prove that they weren't ill, so had instructions to 'have nothing to do with the diarrhoea excuse'. Private Burrage of the Artists' Rifles recalled the time in November 1917 at Dirty Bucket Camp near Poperinghe when a raw American MO was posted to them. Private Dave Barney told him he had visited the latrines twenty-six times in twenty-four hours. Others claimed to be worse than this. The MO called them the 'Charley's Aunts', the title of a long-running play on London's West End. Burrage, unfortunately, was less ambitious, and told the MO he had been seven times in twenty-four hours with the result that the doctor reckoned he was bound up and gave him something to get his bowels moving.

At an aid post near Bapaume in August 1918, an unfortunate Tommy really did have constipation and suffered the indignity of an enema.

The medical orderly used the only syringe available, a solid brass job. Later it was used to clear another man's ear because he couldn't even hear if someone was offering him a drink. The bloke who'd just had the enema shouted at the 'deaf 'un' to let him know where the syringe had been. The man's hearing suddenly improved remarkably.

Some of the infantry arrived in the trenches at night time and then had to dig all night or fill sandbags, sometimes with little or no food. On 23 October 1916 the 2/West Yorkshires had a night of marching under shelling at Le Transloy followed by digging in the trenches till dawn with just a drop of tea. At least the subsequent rations were good.

Frank Dunham and the 25/Londons marched towards the Cambrai front for four days in November 1917 on inadequate rations. However, when they got to Simencourt delayed mail caught up with them. Dunham received three 'very acceptable' parcels. It was difficult for the British Forces Post Office to keep up with units on the move.

By Train

Long journeys by train could also bring hardship. Private Daniel Sweeney (2/Lincolns) was on a train from Rouen from midnight on Friday to 9.15am on Sunday morning in July 1915, and had to survive on a pound of bully beef and six hard biscuits. Luckily he did have a box of chocolates, which he shared with the other men.

Lieutenant Mottram only had iron rations on the journey from Étaples to Poperinghe late in 1915. He was on the train for 'days'. At least he didn't suffer like the 10/Durham Light Infantry: they had to catch a train to Vignacourt early in 1916. They could smell the fresh bread in a boulangerie but could not afford to buy any. Then they had a four-day march to Beauval in freezing snow.

The 2/West Yorkshires marched to a railhead on 21 November 1916. However, their train was delayed several hours and the menu was cold bully beef and biscuits. But Corporal Robinson ('Buggy'), the small fire expert, had other ideas. He conjured up one from a few wood chippings, old letters, envelopes and scraps of newspaper. He applied a match and puffed madly and finally produced a roaring fire. Other men came to marvel at it and to get a light for their own efforts. Buggy cooked a bully beef stew and brewed tea. The train eventually arrived the next day and the officers went into 'first-class' carriages which had broken windows and seats without springs. They had only scraps to eat from their packs. There was a ban on smoking when it got dark in case it helped enemy bombers to pick out the train. Likewise, the engine cabs were covered in.

Trains moved very slowly with frequent stops and some of these lasted so long there was time for officers to nip off to shops and restaurants. Lieutenant Cyril Rawlings (1/Welch) had a journey to the front in 1915 with numerous half-hour halts, during which soldiers made fires and cooked food in their mess tins. On another journey from Rouen in 1915 Private Henry Botton (1/East Surreys) got off at a halt and brewed tea and fried a piece of bacon. Sometimes men were caught out when the train started to move off, often causing them to abandon food and, in a few cases, precious cooking equipment.

Lieutenant Crerar (2/Royal Scots Fusiliers) remembered wayside stalls manned by English ladies. Alfred Burrage described the wild rush for the 'wet' side of the station buffet at Étaples in March 1917. In the first few months of the war French citizens were very generous in handing out food and drink to soldiers in slow-moving trains. On their journey on 13 August 1914 to Rouen the 2/RWF were given wine at every station. John Reith (5/Cameronians) had a similar experience travelling from Le Havre in November 1914, when he received gifts of tea, coffee, peaches and other fruits. Reith, the battalion transport officer, travelled in style. His carriage – which was a horse box – had hay arranged as an armchair, a sofa and a dining area.

Lieutenant-Colonel Arthur Osburn, a senior brigade MO, made frequent rail journeys late in 1914 and noted waste food strewn everywhere by the railway lines. One of his staff even found a sack containing sixty unopened tins of chicken and tongue. Captain Ritchie, a Cameronian, recalled seeing very large quantities of bully beef, cheese, hard biscuits, tea and sugar on trains in 1915. Les Read had no complaints about the plentiful food and drink on a train from Le Havre in July 1915.

Welcome at the Ports

Arriving at the ports from England in 1914 and 1915 was mostly a cheerful business. On 14 August 1914 the 2/Scots Guards arrived at Le Havre and were served by French reservists with pails of strong coffee mixed with rum. There were also tins of sardines – five men to a tin – but the bread was sour and mouldy. Ordinary Seaman Myall, Royal Naval Division, arriving in Antwerp in October 1914, got a tremendous welcome of coffee, loaves of bread and tins of meat. The 6/Queen's Royal West Surreys were in Boulogne in June 1915. As they marched to the railway station they called out cheeky remarks to young women lining the streets to greet them, and the ladies duly screamed enthusiastically, 'Tommee! Tommee!' and tossed sweet biscuits and chocolate to them. The war didn't seem so bad then.

By 1916 far fewer of the offerings were free. Frank Dunham marched from Le Havre to Harfleur on 25 October 1916 and old women offered bottles of wine and beer for sale whilst children begged for ration biscuits. Alfred Burrage's reception in Le Havre in March 1917 was even worse: no one came out to greet them. The tea at the base camp was cold and foul and all there was to eat was a handful of crumbs of bread and hard biscuit tossed on to their mess tins by a filthy little orderly with dirty fingers. As far as Burrage could ascertain, there was no good reason for short rations at a major port with large, well-equipped kitchens.

Moving Artillery and Engineers

The Royal Artillery and the Royal Engineers did not use trains when they journeyed as units because of the amount of weaponry, ordnance and equipment (mobile bridges, for instance) which they had to lug around. The 7th Field Company, Royal Engineers, took twelve days to move from the Somme to Arras in April 1917 during appalling weather. Their equipment was carried on horse-drawn wagons and only some of the sappers had to walk. They called in at a town or large village every day. Doullens and Querrieu, fair-sized towns, had shops, the first the sappers had seen for months (and females). Overnight billets were generally good but not so the rations, and the sappers ate a lot of bully beef and hard biscuits. Sappers often received very good treatment from fellow Engineering units. The 7th relieved the 80th in Hénin on 15 June 1917 and their CO (Major Bremner) made sure that hot tea was ready for the relief as soon as it arrived.

The Artillery regarded themselves as 'nobody's children' because they constituted a brigade not attached to any division; this meant that their supply lines were sometimes less efficient than ordinary divisional ones. The 377 Battery moved a long way south in November 1917 to get to the Cambrai battlefield, carrying six 18-pounder guns, Lewis guns, rifles, equipment for the maintenance of the guns and transport for the horses, their carers and equipment. There was materiel also for signallers – lines, lamps and flags. There were picks, shovels, axes, ropes and canvas for shelters. In addition, there were the normal supplies – rations, water and kitchen wagons.

On this journey in 1917 they had very little food and no iron rations were issued. There was supposed to be an advanced dump from which the QM could collect food for men and horses, but he was informed that it had 'gone astray' and that 'maybe' the train bringing it had broken down. About 100,000 men were on the move towards Cambrai so it was something of a logistical nightmare.

377 officers had to turn a blind eye to their men 'grubbing around' villages to scrounge what they could. In fact, they fared better than the officers, most of whom ate only dry biscuits for a few days. The battery arrived after five days on 16 November virtually starving. At least rations started arriving then, even though it was only bully beef, bread and hot tea. What had arrived safely, however, was the 'caravan'. This was a decrepit ex-gypsy vehicle full of whisky for this whole Artillery Brigade. Its wood was so rotten that it looked likely to collapse at any minute under the weight of hundreds of bottles. There were constant cries of 'Is the caravan all correct?' – a shout that was incorporated into Artillery language generally meaning 'are things going as they should?' The caravan finally disappeared completely: it certainly never arrived for the Battle of Cambrai. What happened to the whisky was not recorded.

Moving Wounded and Sick Soldiers – Aid Posts

There were special communication trenches to carry back badly wounded men on stretchers, but sometimes losses were so high that the stretcher-bearers were forced to use ordinary communication trenches, which could create chaos, with ration parties and others trying to move in the opposite direction. There were originally eighteen stretcher-bearers per battalion but by 1918 there were thirty-two. The stretcher-bearers took the wounded to aid posts, where capability in dealing with the

An *estaminet* in Allery. Drawing by Henry Ogle.

range of wounds inflicted by modern weaponry improved steadily throughout the war, along with the drugs, dressings and equipment.

Frank Dunham was an orderly in an aid post in Ytres. He thought that the wounded and sick were well cared for in terms of food and drink. There was plenty of tea, sugar and milk and a good primus stove to keep up a steady flow of tea. Water (wounded men constantly needed water) was also plentiful. Lieutenant Blacker (4/Coldstream Guards) remembered vividly the mug of tea and sweet biscuits he was handed when he was wounded by the Canal du Nord on 28 September 1918.

In June 1918 Dunham was an orderly in the aid post at Picquiny on the banks of the Somme. There was a canteen next door to provide many extras for the wounded, such as calves'-foot jellies, packets of cornflakes, tins of condensed milk and port wine. Unfortunately, according to Dunham, not all of this reached those for whom it was intended, especially the port.

Medical Stations, Centres and Hospitals

Serious casualties were taken from the aid posts to advanced dressing stations on carts, wheeled stretchers or by horse-drawn or motor ambulances. Second Lieutenant J.S. Tatham (9/King's Royal Rifle Corps) was shot in the leg (February 1916), and at a dressing station Royal Army Medical Corps orderlies gave him some tea and cigarettes.

The next stop was the casualty clearing stations, sometimes by rail. Siegfried Sassoon (2/RWF) was taken to the CCS at Warlencourt with a shoulder wound in April 1917. They gave him an anti-tetanus injection and a cup of Bovril.

Urgent surgical cases could be taken to advanced operating centres which were within ten miles of the front. The last step was to a base hospital aboard one of the thirty or more special hospital trains. There were fifty-eight general hospitals, two isolation hospitals and seven convalescent depots and also a mobile path lab.

When John Glubb was badly wounded and put on a hospital train he was too badly hurt to notice much, but he did recall cooks in their tall caps and white coats working in a very large and well-equipped kitchen. J.S. Tatham described his train as 'beautiful'. He was asked what he would like to eat, and there was plenty of whisky and beer.

Sustenance in Hospitals

On hospital food and drink there were differing reports. In 1915 Private Read of the 17/Leicesters was in hospital in Rouen and the breakfast eggs were fresh from a Devon farm (its name was scribbled on them). He 'lived off the fat of the land', literally showered with fruit and chocolates. When he got back to the Leicesters at Warluzel, looking for more rest before he was back in the trenches, he sat on a cart in the spring (1916) sunshine peeling spuds and cutting up meat for a stew. An obliging hen fluttered by and laid an egg.

The wounded and sick received gift parcels paid for by donations collected in the West Indies. These had Cadbury's chocolates in nice boxes and one tough guardsman was rather affronted by these and flung a box away, shouting, 'I'm a soldier!' Lieutenant Colonel Osburn of the 46th Field Ambulance in 1915 said that pneumonia cases in his hospital were fed on chicken broth and tumblers of egg flip with plenty of sugar and brandy. Lance-Corporal John Jackson was in this hospital in January 1916 for a week and reported that he had plenty of good, plain food. In February Jackson was in another hospital of marquees near Lillers. Meals were extremely punctual – breakfast at 7am, dinner at 12.30, tea at 4pm and cocoa at 6.30pm.

But there was a different tale from Captain Robert Graves (1/RWF) in July 1916. He was wounded on the 21st and was taken to hospital at Heilly. There was no fresh milk for the tea and Graves detested condensed milk. All the water had to be boiled. There was no fruit although one doctor brought him two unripe greengages. Graves whispered to him that he would get him a whole orchard of greengages when he recovered. At this time his mother was informed that he was dead.

George Coppard (37 Machine-Gun Company) said that the food in the hospital at Le Chateau de Chocques was good (April 1916). Private Beecham of 1/Hull Pals at No. 1 Australian Hospital in Wimereux ate excellent chicken and drank stout every day. Second Lieutenant Tatham had been there the previous February and was 'deluged' with fruit and other food. Captain Jack was in the 24th Field Ambulance Hospital in March 1916 end enjoyed champagne and port – and so did the orderlies.

Sergeant Char Beechey of the 8/Royal Fusiliers did not record what he thought of his hospital food just before Christmas 1916, but he seemed relieved that he had a parcel containing mince pies and pork pies and State Express cigarettes. He shared all this with his fellow patients. Alfred Burrage was in hospital in May 1917 near Arras suffering from trench fever (he had not yet been in a trench). Like Robert Graves he intensely disliked tinned milk. Because of his condition this was his sole diet; it put him off the stuff completely. One day he heard that there was Burton's Bass beer in the hospital canteen, but by the time he got there it was all gone. In St Omer Hospital my father could also have no solid food for three weeks when he caught Spanish flu in 1918.

Alfred Burrage had a bad time during the German offensive of 1918. By 9 April his feet were horribly swollen. They took him to a Canadian hospital where he had nothing to eat all day. A nurse asked him if he had any complaints about the food. Fred Dunham heard reports about poor food in the hospital at Valenciennes in March 1918.

If wounded men could walk unaided they were expected to make their own way to the various medical posts. Lieutenant Leslie Yorath Sanders suffered a superficial wound on his right shoulder during 1917 on Hill 60. A dressing was applied to this and he then joined a crowd of men walking to Ypres, which was several miles away. He broke off his journey to take coffee in a café before continuing to the hospital in the city.

Fifteen

Egg and Chips in the *Estaminets*

Estaminets

It didn't take many months of the war for French and Belgian citizens to realise that there was money to be made by selling food and drink to British soldiers. In the village of Maroeuil in November 1917 it was estimated that there were sixty-five *estaminets*. An *estaminet* was a small café. The word may well have come from the German word 'stamen', a post for a cow to be tied to whilst it was at the trough. This suggested a rather basic establishment. If the residents of a house or cottage were feeding themselves, why not extend this to paying customers? They could make extra coffee or tea and sell their surplus wine or beer, either home-made or bought in. What they learnt very soon was that Tommy especially desired eggs and chips (*pommes de terre frites* – translated by Tommy as 'Bombardier Fritz' or 'Pompadour Fritz').

The *estaminet* was a traditional concept long before Tommy appeared on the scene but the number of them increased rapidly in 1915 in the British sector. The *estaminet* now expanded its takeaway services, being just as happy to sell items such as sweet biscuits, chocolates and sweets as well as cooked food. When the Artists' Rifles arrived in Bavincourt in March 1917 there was hardly a dwelling with nothing for sale. The residents were equally disposed to let Tommy take away raw eggs and potatoes to cook himself. Private Dave Barney, Artists' Rifles, was somewhat suspicious of Bavincourt's 'Madame Tindrawers's' black-encrusted frying pan and preferred to cook his own.

The *estaminet* adopted myriad forms, one of which was run from a cottage by two incredibly old and decrepit women on the Ypres–Brielen road just west of the Yser Canal. The trenches were just on the other side of the canal (1915). There were no other civilians within miles. Vlamertinghe, the nearest village, had long been deserted. The crones supplied coffee to the nearby artillery, or whoever, and were making a fortune for their old age.

Some were large establishments, probably pre-dating the war, employing several people cooking and serving, very often attractive young females, and using two or more stoves. But, however grand, they were not restaurants – in the sense of having an extensive menu prepared by chefs. They were not even proper cafés – businesses with specialist premises which were not primarily someone's home. In the same way, an *estaminet* was not a real shop.

Estaminets were modest places where Tommy could sit on a chair or a bench, eat at a table in a warm room, clink glasses of 'plonk' or 'van blong' with a pal and mutually mutter 'bon chance' or 'bon santé'. To him it was a 'just-a-minute', an indication of its prority: as far as Tommy was concerned being in an *estaminet* was his number one choice and anything else had to wait, including the war.

Difficult Choices

With so many *estaminets* nearby, Tommy sometimes had to make difficult choices. Moving up to the Ypres Salient in September 1917 the Artists' Rifles were on the Franco-Belgian border; and the *estaminet* at Houtkerque was dull and the one at Watou was lively. It was either a quiet evening in Belgium sitting round a warm stove and supping coffee in someone's kitchen, or a piano and a sing-song and some dirty jokes in France. *Estaminets* in Armentières in 1915 competed to provide the best entertainment, particularly after the Military Police had gone to bed. If you kept quiet you could break the curfew.

Similarly, the range on offer in Beuvry in March 1916 went from quiet to 'cabaret'. In an example of the latter 2/RWF's 'conjuror' performed tricks and unprintable songs for ten francs a night and free drinks. He was the sort of chap who sung 'Somewhere the sun is shining' when it was pelting down cats and dogs in the trench.

Some *estaminets*, indeed, were positively Rabelasion and some even offered prostitution, or at least very friendly girls. Others had a family atmosphere and superior food and drink. There might be a large central table, perhaps seating up to ten of the noisiest customers, but small side tables for quieter men, perhaps engaged in writing a letter home and drinking coffee rather than beer or wine. You paid up as soon as you got your frothless and spineless French beer. Someone calculated he needed 242 mugs of the stuff to become really drunk. A bowl of tea or coffee at the price of a penny was often preferred.

'Madame Tindrawers's' French beer in Bavincourt was a pale dandelion colour with only the faintest flavour of beer. There were also jugs of 'English' beer but the only real difference was the price – four pence a glass (the French stuff was one pence a glass). Down the road 'Madame Cow' had the best coffee, bread and butter in the village. There was enormous competition amongst the various establishments. Another cottage had delicious petit buerre biscuits for sale. Eggs and bread were in plentiful supply everywhere. The wine was of indeterminate origin and colour. Lance-Corporal Mountford of the 10/Royal Fusiliers visited three *estaminets* in the village where he was billeted and rated them about equal – thin beer sour as vinegar, insipid van blong and cognac. But in one of them he discovered some half-decent claret, but it was 1.75 franc a bottle, more than a day's pay for most Tommies.

Character and Characters

It tended to be very cosy in an *estaminet* – low ceilings, fuggy atmosphere, a stove in an alcove leading to the kitchen, some shelves holding dusty, primitively labelled bottles of no particular vintage. Soup could be in pots on the stove making it even warmer. Oil lamps cast a dim, friendly glow. Some of them were really shabby affairs. When the 2/RWF were passing through Beuvry on 2 March 1916 there was a place named 'La Gaieté'. The slovenly and dirty owner was outside suckling an unwashed child with another scrabbling in the muddy road. Beside her was an unshaven ASC man in an unbuttoned coat and wearing his cap on the back of his unkempt head. It was claimed that ASC personnel had a lot to do with *estaminet* owners.

With the character of *estaminets* came the characters, like the 2/RWF 'conjuror'. Alfred Burrage and Dave Barney and another mate were the 'Three-must-get-beers' at an *estaminet* near Dirty Bucket Camp (Poperinghe 1917). There were communication problems before the development of 'franglais'. Private Bobett squatted down, flapped imaginary wings and squawked if he wanted eggs. He pretended to slice for bacon and said 'moo moo' for milk, but had trouble in making it clear he wanted some boot polish. The best system for remembering the French for egg was to think of a horse and go 'Hoof'.

Scots soldiers had trouble with the order "twa egg and chips'. The French thought they were saying 'trois' and gave them three eggs instead of two. Getting along with the French was a bit of a strain for some Old Contemptibles. Dick Richards (2/RWF) had a friend called Billy who tried to order a bottle of wine in a mixture of English, Hindustani and Chinese plus a French phrase (not 's'il vous plait'). The French response to anything like this was 'No compris', whereupon Billy – again in English, Hindustani and Chinese – threatened to land one on him. Billy's view of foreigners was that they all needed a good bashing. The Fusiliers' last view of Billy was of him riding down the Champs Élysée accompanied by two of these foreigners – of the young and female variety. He got a Blighty One.

A Spot of Trouble

Military Police tried to be on hand to stop fights and damage to property, and to persuade Tommy to go back to his billet or camp at the required time. They also might sniff coffee or tea mugs in case illicit whisky was being consumed (with a nod and a wink from the owner), spirits being banned for other ranks, or if there was stolen rum in the red wine. In these circumstances, it was just as well that Tommy didn't bring along his rifle and a few rounds of ammunition. In the early days of the war it was part of their 'walking out' dress, and when they were well-oiled they were prone to taking pot shots at passing aircraft or birds, or the glasses and windows in the *estaminet* and even the carcasses hanging up in the butcher's shop.

Fights were not uncommon. My father was in an *estaminet* in Contay in September 1917 (he was there helping to cut down the wood which was needed for trench and road duckboards and fascines – also put on the front of tanks to help them across trenches and ditches). He was accompanied by two friends, Joe and Steve, who were champion boxers. Some Canadian ex-lumberjacks (there to supervise the cutting down) were in the *estaminet*. One of them knocked over Joe's beer and refused to replace it, resulting in a wild free-for-all. The COs of both units put all *estaminets* out of bounds for a while on pain of eight days of Field Punishment No. 1, which included no pay and an exclusive diet of bully beef and biscuits.

On Offer and Prices

Although coffee, beer and wine were the staple liquid refreshment on offer there were other tipples. Private Henry Ogle had a choice of red or white wine, hot or cold, grenadine, Malaga (sweet raisin wine) and a non-alcoholic drink called 'Byorh'. Sergeant Read liked the citron on sale in Bailleuval. At Berles-au-Bois this was used as a syrup in red and white wine – so was grenadine.

Estaminets had names a bit like English pubs – 'Au Lion Blanc', 'Écu de France', 'Reine d'Anglais', 'Au Trois Empereurs'. 'Rendez-vous' was common, as you would expect. The names of saints were also often used. Other notable titles were 'Vrai Coeur joyeux', 'Coin minteur', 'Le Soleil lui pour le Monde', L'Habitude' and 'Le Nid du Rat'. 'L'Hirondelle' and 'Au chants des Oiseaux' were from nature-lovers.

Tommy was less interested in their names than what was on offer inside and what it cost. Soldiers would visit a variety of establishments while in France and Flanders and the universal opinion was that most prices were reasonable but that over-charging became more common as the war proceeded. Complaints became more strident than satisfaction. Even in 1915 Robert Graves criticised the lack of French hospitality as villages around Béthune made a lot of money from the 100,000 or so men billeted in the area.

Second Lieutenant Ian Melhuish of the 7/Somerset Light Infantry wrote on 26 July 1915 that the French were very pleasant. Something must then have happened because on 11 August he wrote that the much-vaunted generosity of the French was on the wane and their chief object was to make as much money as possible from British soldiers

– especially those who were newly arrived, and possibly naive. Harold Beechey was in Merville in November 1916 enjoying the cafés and *estaminets*, but in December, in another village, he was shocked by the prices demanded for goods such as sardines, sweet biscuits, chocolate and tinned fruit – three francs a tin when Tommy's daily pay was between a third and two-thirds of that.

In Bus-les-Artois, also in 1916, villagers were charging high prices but were losing a lot of cups and spoons when the Hull Commercials were there. But in many diaries were tales of free food and drink when there had been a lot of casualties – men missing who had become great friends of *estaminet* proprietors.

What Tommy could Afford

Basic pay for a private from 1914–17 was a shilling a day. But there were higher pay grades for privates: a first-class private such as Dick Richards of the 2/RWF was paid one shilling and seven pence, and this went up to two shillings a day in late 1917 (one shilling and three pence for ordinary privates). However, deductions were made for allotments to wives or families, for barrack damages or lost kit and for disciplinary reasons. So instead of picking up ten shillings or more every ten days (around twelve francs) Tommy might get only five francs. Indeed, Private Daniel Sweeney (2/Lincolns) remembered getting only five francs a month: he either had a poor memory or he had several wives and families.

How far would Tommy's food and drink budget go? On fourteen francs for ten days (maybe seven francs of which was saved whilst on the front line) he wouldn't expect to have egg and chips and a bottle of wine or beer every night. Even on twenty francs it was touch and go. Perhaps he could only drink coffee on some nights or stay in the billet on some nights: he still had his ration food and drink. But it was not much fun staying in on your own while your chums went out on the town. This calculation also does not take into account takeaway purchases of cigarettes, coffee, bread, eggs, sweet biscuits, chocolate and tins of food (there was heavy reliance on parcels for these items).

An important source of extra money was postal orders from home – a sort of non-personalised cheque which Tommy could exchange for cash in a post office. But if he was daft (or desperate) enough to use one in an *estaminet* (there might be no post office nearby and he was desperate for a drink) it was heavily discounted – ten per cent or even more. This situation got worse in late 1917 as the rise in food and drink prices since 1914 – around 150 per cent –outstripped pay rises – about thirty-three per cent. If a soldier was asked for a franc for a meal and a franc for a bottle of wine or beer, that would take up his twenty francs every ten days. Married men would fare worse. George Coppard called being 'skinned' (no money) in a village with lots of *estaminets* as 'the apex of misery'.

There were ways of trying to get round these financial difficulties: you could ask for credit at the *estaminet*, let's say against the prospect of a postal order. You could build up a slate but there were limits to how far an *estaminet* owner would let you go. Men did ask for pay advances on pay days but eventually you had to pay it back and there were again limits on this. One soldier, offered a five francs loan, told a very young pay officer to take it back and 'spend it on a f****** rocking horse'.

Again, as with canteens, there was the 'pool' or 'tarpaulin' system. A group of friends could put together all they had and make sure everyone got a meal and a drink. With mates on higher pay you could be on to a good thing, but there was a limit; you had to pay your way in the long run. No one was going to accept a long-term sponger or borrower.

Estaminets Here and There

Estaminets could exist in houses in towns or large villages, cottages and farmhouses and other wayside dwellings. Dick Richards was in a house on the outskirts of Abbéville in November 1916. He bought egg and chips, and that was alright, but the drinks were heavily watered down. In revenge he stole two empty wooden tubs to make a fire and later returned to take some more.

Lieutanant Mottram had the job of adjudicating in cases where Flemish proprietors had complained of alleged criminal behaviour by soldiers in their establishments. Early in 1916 one such owner claimed that one of his customers had not paid enough for a barrel of beer. Mottram was able to make a deal with him and this included a nice meal for himself of chicken, salad, hare pâté, jam, gingerbread and excellent red wine. In another case the owner said that he knew the regiment of men whom he accused of bad behaviour because they had inadvertently left behind a sack marked with the name 'O.A.T.S.'

In January 1915, at Bois Grenier, an *estaminet* (the 'Cheval') was so near the front line that the 2/RWF could enjoy beer and chips in the midst of repairing trenches. A girl even came out from the 'Cheval' to sell chocolate directly to them in the trench. It was a pretty quiet front. An *estaminet* on the edge of Armentières (February 1915) was so near the communication trenches that the 2/RWF could slip out for beer and carry it back in rum jars pretending it was water. Wine bottles were also brought back in sandbags. Dick Richards said that these were great days of cheap, good wine but slowly the quality dropped and the price rose. The *estaminet* they were visiting was simply a 'domestic shop'. Private John Jackson (6/Cameronians) remembered villages just behind the lines in the ruined village of Mazingarde which he could reach from the trenches for eggs and bread and much else. At this time (September 1915) his five francs pay was worth three shillings and eight pence. This rate of exchange of about nine to ten pence a franc remained fairly static throughout the war – between twenty-four and twenty-eight francs for a pound.

Little Gems

Estaminets could be perfect little gems, such as the unpretentious cottage at St Valery-sur-Somme in late 1917, which sold top-rate coffee, rolls and butter, or, if you preferred, some cider. Walk a little further down the road and there was another cottage cooking delicious fried eggs. Private Dick Read loved the cottage (December 1915) where he drank coffee and cognac and took away nice chocolates and sweet biscuits, all served by the equally delicious Émilienne, who would allow you to pay the next day or open up a slate.

Farmhouses could be in idyllic surroundings. Winston Groom and his machine-gun team sat in an orchard near Arras in April 1917 on a lovely evening (the weather had changed dramatically from earlier in the month). They had a table and chairs under an apple tree. They had brought their own alcohol but Madame was preparing a chicken for them. Unfortunately, when the cooked bird arrived its head and neck were still attached and there seemed to be a distinct possibility that its innards were intact as well. Whether this woman was new to farming (or cooking) was not clear. Groom stuck his knife in it and held it aloft, singing the soldiers' chorus from *Faust*. It was all bones and great lumps of fat. 'No bon?' asked Madame sadly. The situation was saved by some fat pork and they sat there under the trees having a very peaceful and serene evening.

John Jackson was riding with other battalion cyclists to Lillers on 15 December 1915. They stopped at a wayside *estaminet* and drank wine and shared a large cake he had got in a parcel. Corkage was never charged: you could take in what you liked to an *estaminet* as long as you spent some money.

Converted Billets

Billets easily evolved into *estaminets*. All it was necessary to do was put up a notice reading 'Eggs, fish, chips, tea, stout' – even get an Army clerk to print it for you. As Captain Billy Nevill entered Ribemont village in September 1915 there was one such notice – 'English beer sold whole-sale, jam, fruit, fresh butter, milk'. This cheered him up tremendously. When he had gone up to the trenches east of Albert in the previous month he had taken with him a good stock of fresh milk, wine and eggs from his billet. Now it looked like he was going to be lucky once again.

The 2/RWF had less pleasant memories of billets in Cardonette (July 1916) with rapacious citizens even over-charging their fellow French-men, who were very poorly paid, as an extension of fleecing Tommy. Bruce Bairnsfather called his billet in Flanders 'Fleecem', in deference to Flemish spelling. His hostess stole their bully beef and biscuits to use as payment in kind to an epileptic working for her (December 1914).

Cafés

Cafés varied greatly. They were places built as businesses and not prima-rily homes, unless there had been a considerable conversion. The types of café frequented by Robert Graves and Dick Richards were very differ-ent. Graves was in the 'Globe' in the early afternoon of 15 October 1915 drinking champagne cocktails. Officers' cafés were more like restaurants –

The YMCA hut in Sailly-sur-la-Lys. Drawing by Henry Ogle.

very elegant establishments. Richards was in a café near Albert playing 'Crown and Anchor'. He won a vast sum in this game in July 1916. However, the spending spree which followed was distinctly officer-like. He bought fifty bottles of champagne at twelve francs a bottle and he and his mates lived royally off these for a month or more. He wasn't so lucky earlier in the year, having been caught drinking in a café after an 8pm curfew. He got eight days of Field Punishment No. 1 which, as an old soldier, he regarded as lenient.

Stalls

Like the girl selling chocolates in the trenches at Bois Grenier in January 1915, and the children selling bread in Poperinghe in 1917, the French and the Flemish were prepared to bring food and drink to Tommy for sale. Frank Dunham recalled a Belgian family next to the YMCA hut in an Army camp late in 1916 selling coffee and other drinks and cigarettes, and doing very well out of it from the thousands of soldiers there. Villagers also set up stalls in the enormous base camp at Étaples selling fruit, chocolates and the 'eternal' spearmint (chewing gum), which the stallholders thought was Tommy's staple diet.

Generous Hosts

There was a great deal of goodwill and generosity from French and Flemish citizens. Despite the greed of some of their countrymen, the general impression left on Tommy was that these were good people. Major Walter Vignoles wrote home in February 1916 about a mother and daughter whose house had been struck by two shells, but they refused to move in order to maintain their chicken run and sell eggs and coffee to British soldiers.

Some of the French and Flemish who billeted troops were ready to use their billeting fees not only for accommodation but also to make the generous provision of frequent meals and drinks for no extra charge. Madame in the large farmhouse at Agnez-les-Duisains (10 April 1917) was the host of Captain John Glubb for the night as he made his way with the 7th Field Company, Royal Engineers, to the Battle of Arras.

She had 'a heart of gold', according to Glubb, constantly stoking up the fire in the kitchen (it was snowing outside) and producing fresh eggs and coffee.

In Le Havre in August 1914 enormous quantities of beautifully cooked food and excellent wine were recalled by Lieutenant Rowland Owers (2/Duke of Wellingtons). Others in the port around this time had similar gastronomic experiences: Captain James Patterson, adjutant of the 1/South Wales Borderers, had plum brandy: Sapper Hugh Bellow was treated to all types of luxuries, especially superb bread.

The officers of the 1/Cameronians were on the Aisne on 4 October 1914 in a chateau owned by a Spanish nobleman. He was lavish with his wine (but drew the line at shooting some of the pigeons in his towers). Two weeks later they were in a billet in Vlamertinghe and every morning their Belgian hosts sent in a tray of liqueurs. Les Read, a private in July 1915, marched all night from Watten to Houlle but then had to stand guard for hours. He was amazed when a girl turned up with a basin of steaming hot coffee and a long, narrow slice of fresh crusty bread.

Lieutenant Guy Chapman (13/Royal Fusiliers) recalled a generous housewife south of Arras in St Anard, in February 1916, bringing to the officers' mess a vast dish of cooked eggs flanked by two bottles of Nuits. Henry Ogle remembered a converted farmhouse at Allery (October 1916) owned by an Englishman, who put wine, cake, cigarettes and cigars on the supper table. Winston Groom (London Rifle Brigade) was in the upper part of a barn in Paradis late in 1916, but it was very dry and packed with clean straw. Even better was the nightly arrival of the farmer's wife with newly cooked bread (a practice soon to be banned by the French authorities).

In a large farmhouse at Allouagne (May 1916) near Lillers there were several barns which were used as billets, but the daughter of the house went round to each one with enormous slices of bread she had made herself, laden with lashings of creamy butter, also produced on the farm. George Coppard and other members of the 37 Machine-Gun Company helped to make some more, pouring milk into barrels with rods through them and oscillating them by pulling cords.

Frank Dunham – then a cyclist in the 25/Londons (January 1918) – had ten lovely days in an old woman's house at Ribemont – good meat, eggs, fish, potatoes, and on one night a chicken which had been selected by Dunham and his pals and even plucked by them. In May of 1918

Dunham also did well – in a farmhouse (which also provided the battalion post room) – being supplied with coffee and food all day long.

Second Lieutenant Read (4/Royal Sussex) in a billet in Rouville in August 1918 ate omelettes 'fit for the Gods' accompanied by salad and slices of home-made bread loaded with country butter – a nice change from tinned fare. A bowl of delicious coffee followed and then he settled down to smoke his favourite blend with his favourite pipe. He had come a long way since 1915 when he was just Private Read. Actually, what he regarded as his best billet of all was as a sergeant in the 17/Leicesters at Christmas 1916 in the Pas de Calais – enormous meals, plenty of beer and the presence of some young ladies. Also in 1916 there was 'Tante' near Arras in her lovely and cosy kitchen – fresh milk from her cows (milked by one of Read's pals) instead of the dreadful 'Ideal' milk. Sitting around the table in the kitchen drinking coffee and cognac was a dream of civilised existence. Supper to follow consisted of fried eggs and cocoa and sometimes welsh rarebit made with the Leicesters' cheese rations.

Troops could be making just a one-night stop as they passed through towards or from the front but, as in John Glubb's case, the hospitality could be just as good as if they were staying longer. Some Tommies actually took the initiative and called at houses which were not official billets to ask for food and drink and were nearly always made welcome. Private Archie Surfleet couldn't praise the villagers in Neuf Berquin too highly. They were ushered into the best room in a house and presented with a lovely meal. The hosts adamantly refused any payment.

Sixteen

Beer and Wine

Weak Beer

English beer was normally available in EF canteens. Many *estaminets* also offered 'English beer' but Tommy was going to be lucky if it really was. He was still going to be charged more for it than local beer and it was not going to be much stronger. Captain J.C. Dunn, MO of the 2/RWF, recalled that French soldiers were surprised that their English counterparts could afford any but the weakest beer – the French couldn't. Indeed, a small Bass cost a shilling in July 1915, a day's pay for Tommy.

The very weak French beer sold at around a penny a glass. There were various estimates from Tommy of how much you needed of this stuff to get you drunk, ranging from seventy-two glasses to over 200! But if there was nothing else available, or anything you could afford, French it had to be. French breweries had to rapidly expand their rate of production to keep up with the rising demand. The one at Estaires trebled its output between August 1914 and July 1915.

Unscrupulous breweries could make even more money by further watering down already anaemic beer. In Béthune in October 1915 they were pumping extra water into it through hosepipes. *Estaminets* were prone to adding even more water. Sometimes they mixed this stuff with equally pale and acidic white wine. A café in Bois Grenier even served up 'stout', half of which was watered-down French beer. It was Dick Richards and his mates who were drinking it and fondly thinking of English beer.

Yet the Old Contemptibles of 1914, like Richards, were accustomed to weak beer or 'swipes' from wet Army canteens. This was designed to control drunkenness, given the alcoholic capacities of these veterans (and to make a tidy profit). This policy tended to continue during the war and was extremely popular with French brewers. So the CO of the 15/Londons was happy to provide 'light' French beers in the support lines for his men in October 1918, in the knowledge that it was not much different from drinking water.

Not much Beer in the Trenches

Nearly all the beer, however, was restricted to the back areas. The small number of cases where it appeared in the trenches all occurred on quiet fronts. The 2/West Yorkshires got local beer when on brigade support at Nurlu in March 1917 but this was at a time when the Germans were retreating to the Hindenburg Line. Therefore, Tommy mainly had to forgo his beer in the trench and just dream of it to come in the rest areas. Wilfred Owen wrote home rather wistfully on 4 January 1916 that he would gladly swap his meat ration for a mug of English beer.

The New Armies of 1915 and later became resigned to the lack of decent beer and moved more and more to van blong, even though that was pretty weak, too. The officers' messes of the 2/RWF at the end of 1916 assumed that most officers wanted beer, but the picture a year later had changed dramatically – forty per cent in one company preferred coffee and thirty per cent and twenty-five per cent in others.

Some Decent Beer

There were isolated cases of reasonable French beer. Guy Chapman drank from 'misty' bottles in a cool cave in Hesdin in August 1917. The beer discovered by 2nd Lieutenant Guy Chapman (13/Royal Fusiliers) near the station in Boulogne on 31 July 1915 was 'commendable'. John Glubb also obtained good home-brewed beer from a farmhouse kitchen near Vlamertinghe, although that was Flemish beer (8 February 1916). Lieutenant A.H. Crerar (2/Royal Scots Fusiliers) had a similar experience at Montbernondon: plenty of good beer from a pump at the side of the midden. There were monastic sources: the priory at St Sixte was a provider until early in 1916 when the prior refused to sell any more to soldiers when the Royal Engineers pumped out his pond, which he was using to keep up with the demand for his product.

Beer featured prominently in special occasions such as sports days, horse shows and football matches. The winners of a football tournament held amongst the companies of the 12/East Surreys in July 1917 at Roukloshille received a barrel of stout. When Corporal George Coppard won the divisional sack race, one of his prizes was beer provided by HQ staff officers (1 June 1917). Manly contests, especially involving old soldiers, naturally featured beer. In Béthune billets in September 1915 one veteran won a bet that he could drink six large glasses of beer taking only one breath between each one.

Wine Becomes the Staple Diet

A ration issue of wine was rare for the British soldiers – the French soldiers got a bottle a day (when things were going well). Alfred Burrage could recall only one issue during the war and that was during the hectic retreat of March 1918, when his battalion of the Artists' Rifles received a bottle of red wine each. This was probably due to the fact that canteen stocks of wine were liable to fall into the hands of the enemy unless somebody drank it first.

However, wine quickly became a staple diet for Tommy. This was a remarkable change in his drinking habits because the BEF of 1914 was a beer-drinking Army. The relative shortage of English beer and good native beers meant that Tommy was more or less forced over to *vin ordinaire*, or 'van blong', as he called it. They quickly got used to drinking it despite its doubtful quality: it was plentiful and cheap (sometimes a penny a glass) – but what this tasted like was anybody's guess. They could fool themselves they were getting tipsy (it tended to have more alcohol in it than French beer) and were able to forget the war for a while. They got into the habit of drinking as much of it as they could afford. Other ranks were banned from drinking spirits, which were very expensive, in any case. A bottle of whisky would set back Tommy a week's pay. Some still managed somehow to get a drop or two of it, perhaps slipped into their van blong or coffee.

Good Wines

There were fine French wines about but they were beyond Tommy's pocket. Occasionally there were generous gifts of good wine from hosts, but generally not up to the standard of the 1878 vintage presented to Captain Billy Nevill in billets at Tambour in December 1915. In Arras in August 1917 the claims department – which settled cases of compensation for citizens – wheedled burgundy from the owners of some ancient cellars. The deal was that other deep cellars in the city would be protected from looters. In the same month staff officers in Hesdin also enjoyed an alcoholic concoction prepared by the Assistant Provost Marshal of the Highland Division from a battery of nine good wines. After a second glass of this stuff Guy Chapman fell into a deep sleep.

Red wine was usually available in *estaminets* but tended to be more expensive, especially if the owner was putting a drop of grenadine or rum in it. Such munificence could also materialise from a better class of prostitute – a nice drop of something before a nice bit of something else, which was the experience of a very young artillery officer in Dunkirk on 18 June 1917.

Unexpected treasures of wine came into their own during the rapid retreats of 1914 and 1918. August 1914 was a particularly good time for abandoned cellars well-stocked in pre-war times. Men of the Scottish Horse were quickly removed from the duty of guarding such a hoard and replaced by Irish troops. These spent the whole night shooting into barrels of wine to get a good drink, with the result that the beds finished up floating in the stuff. One company discovered hundreds of bottles of red and white in a farmhouse, plus port, champagne and a dozen barrels of beer. Because the retreat from Mons was over they were able to spend several nights doing justice to the collection.

On 9 September 1914, as the front line began to atrophy in Buzancy near the Aisne, RSM Boreham of the 2/RWF spotted a well-stocked sideboard in a stately home during the daylight hours and returned under cover of darkness in stockinged feet to make his presence felt.

However, someone else had the same idea and was engaged in drinking champagne. The RSM was thus forced to make a second attempt but he discovered that the first visitor had scoffed or pinched the lot.

By 24 April 1918 the Germans were still trying to break through. Their objectives that day were the villages of Villers Bretonneux and Hangast. The attack on the former was successful, but the Australian force which had been driven back had been making use of some very good cellars in the area. Enraged at the thought of losing all that fine wine they launched a furious and wild counter-attack and won back their cellars before the enemy could make inroads into them.

There were other times during the war when vintage treasures were uncovered and in quite unexpected locations. Tommy didn't expect to find wine when digging trenches but this is what happened to the 2/RWF in July 1915 in the Laventie sector. The Fusiliers were filling up sandbags when they came across several chests full of wine and champagne packed in straw. Dick Richards was quickly on the spot, as you can imagine. He and his platoon became totally inebriated but a sympathetic lieutenant decided to let them get away with it since it was a very quiet front. Similarly, Lieutenant Vaughan (1/8/Royal Warwickshires) and some fellow officers found a large dump of wine buried in a farmyard ditch in Péronne on 26 April 1917, and the bottles found their way into the mess in ones and twos in order not to arouse suspicion (you were not supposed to steal wine belonging to civilians even if it was just hanging about).

In May 1917 in Marielière, on the St Quentin–Amiens road, men of the 1/Cameronians found a barrel of white wine. Since they were on the move they had to fill up every container they possessed, even the large ones on the mobile kitchen as well as dixies and water bottles, without arousing suspicion on the part of the officers. However, when parade was called the smell of wine was so overpowering that the bounty could not be hidden any longer. Everyone was searched for wine and their train was delayed whilst the inspection proceeded. Guilty men were given field punishments.

Plenty of van blong was available to the 7th Field Company, Royal Engineers, at Monart on 10 March 1917. The result was very loud singing until the early hours and their stern CO banned such spontaneous concerts. Wine could also lead to other artistic outpourings. Private Joyce, barber to the 13/Royal Fusiliers, was reckoned to be sixty years of age. Getting well sozzled with van blong he danced on the cobble-stones at Bailleul with wild abandon. Later in 1916 he got a Blighty One: whether this was following another performance on the cobbles or an accident with his scissors was not recorded.

As Lieutenant Colonel Rowland Fielding and his 15/Londons prepared to assault the enemy on 8 September 1918, the divisional general sent up a couple of bottles of Veuve Cliquot 1906 to the officers' mess. It was the last of the general's purchases from threatened canteens during the March retreat near Épernay. But Fielding gave the champagne to the company commanders and they handed it on to their sergeants. Two months later there was something to celebrate.

Seventeen

Tommy Enterprises

Scroungers

'Perambulating stomachs' also indulged in other initiatives for food and drink – they soon learnt to be thieves or scroungers. The Old Contemptibles were born to these arts and taught the ropes to the new recruits. Farms and smallholdings, for instance, provided endless opportunities for free fresh eggs, vegetables, milk, honey, and even the occasional chicken. Dick Richards, that old soldier of the 2/RWF, bought two chickens from a farm for Christmas celebrations in 1915 and stole seven more at the same time while the farmer wasn't looking.

When Guy Chapman assumed command over some machine-gunners in September 1915 he discovered that one of them was an experienced poacher. He could wring a chicken's neck without the ghost of a sqawk from the bird whilst his fellow machine-gunners engaged the roost owner in polite conversation. When the 4/Coldstream Guards left one billet the *patronne* praised them as the best soldiers she had accommodated because they stole so few eggs and no chickens whatsoever.

In the early war years, landladies, housewives and farmers' wives were more likely to complain about missing chickens. The 1/Cameronians at Marisy St Geneviève in October 1914 were ordered to pay compensation to a landlady for stolen chickens (presumed dead). But as the war progressed these women were more inclined to simply raise prices, so extortion was justified in some cases – a bit of give and take.

The disappearance of eggs was a common occurrence. Lieutenant-Colonel Osburn, CO of the 14 Corps Field Ambulance (July 1915), heard many complaints from Flemish farmers located close to the rest camp near Poperinghe. But old soldiers were never at a loss for an explanation. Private Brown said that he had spotted a hole in a fence and put his hand through it as an act of sheer curiosity. Amazingly, his hand came into direct contact with an egg which had just been laid. He removed it in an attempt to let the farmer have it while it was still warm. His CO asked why he was running when the farmer overtook him and Private Brown assured him he was just desperate to keep the egg as warm as possible for the farmer. 'He said some 'orrible things to me, sir,' complained Brown. 'I think 'e's a German spy, sir.'

The 1/Hull Pal had a terrific time in fields near Hazebrouck in July 1918. It was an area virtually untouched by the war – whole fields of potatoes and peas awaiting harvest. They went very nicely with the piglets genuinely bought from the farmer. In contrast, the 12/East Surreys, foraging for peas in July 1917, were docked a franc each from their pay. In the same month in Berles-au-Bois, the 1/8/Royal Warwickshires escaped fines for vanishing potatoes and other root crops by adopting night-time commando tactics, crawling prone across the ground to avoid detection. Locals in Poperinghe in December 1917 didn't care about disappearing parsnips because they had too many of them and it was nearly Christmas, but a civilian in Houplines in December 1914 was really upset when some of his pigeons vanished from a loft in his farm – they were his pets. Since the 2/RWF had been scrounging wine, champagne, ducks and chickens from him and neighbouring farms, he had good reason to think they were also to blame for his missing pigeons.

Pigeons, indeed, were a favourite delicacy for Tommy. In the item 'Things we want to know', in the first edition of *The Wipers Times* (12 February 1916), there was an enquiry about the name of the brunette infantry officer whose men had got hold of some carrier pigeons and cooked them. And who were his guests? Another question concerned a 200-pound pig 'discovered' on 10 November 1914 at Cordonnerie. It produced only two dixies of pork for the 2/RWF. Another similar animal also 'discovered' a few days earlier had provided enough for a whole company. At this time, moreover, potatoes had been just lying about in the fields and there seemed to be chickens and eggs everywhere. Now they seemed to have all gone.

Fresh milk was always in demand. In a pretty little village on the River Scarpe west of Arras in the summer of 1917, Dave Barney of the Artists'

Rifles noticed a very fat and productive cow. Subsequently, the farmer found it empty of milk at dawn when it had been full the previous evening. This happened for several days until he decided to maintain a watch all night. As a result, he was on hand to apprehend Dave just as his hand was closing around a teat. Dave was philosophical as usual. 'Milk – very bon,' he muttered. 'Trés bon', he added before making a quick getaway. Perhaps Lance-Corporal John Jackson had more of an excuse. He had been out all day on signalling training during the same summer and spotted a cow in a field. He had fresh milk that day rather than the 'Ideal' variety.

Orchards

At the right time of year, passing or resting near orchards was a source of severe temptation for the British soldier. In the sunny September of 1914 the 4/Irish Dragoon Guards, and presumably many other passing units, helped themselves to peaches, nectarines, pears, apricots, apples and bush fruit of many varieties. In the fields near Arras in the summer of 1916 there were raspberries, redcurrants and strawberries in deserted market gardens. Lieutenant Tyndale-Biscoe (Royal Horse Artillery) found rhubarb and enjoyed it stewed.

Robert Graves became interested in the gardens of ruined houses with redcurrants and blackcurrants in Vermelles on 24 June 1915. His CSM had the same idea. They started from different ends but when the sergeant-major saw Graves he saluted and left, as it was not etiquette to eat in the presence of an officer. Graves, not wishing to take advantage of this situation, also saluted and left. Both came back later hoping that the other was not around. However, they were, so both saluted and left again. Someone else had the currants.

Billy Nevill and fellow officers certainly thought their luck was in when they encountered 300 metres of apples at Ribemont in September 1915. They had so many apples they started throwing them at one another like children. The 37 Machine-Gun Company discovered damsons, plums and apples at Rivière on 21 August 1916 near their gun post. It was too dangerous to pick the fruit during the day so they planned to come out at night for a feed and collection. But the enemy fired through the trees at half-hourly intervals aware that there might be fruit pickers lurking amongst them. Fortunately, they packed up about 2am. Subsequently

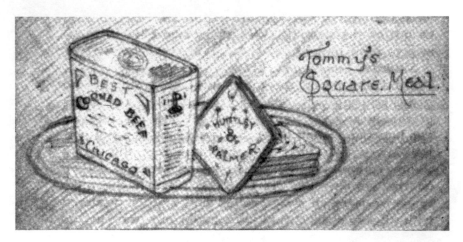

Bully beef and dog biscuits. Drawing by Horace Bruckshaw.

they lit up the trees with flares and pasted them with bullets. In desperation George Coppard and his chums climbed up the trees. Luckily for them, the ploy worked, as the Germans continued to fire low.

A 25/Londons ration party, on a forced detour, found wild raspberries growing in the St Eloi area on 14 July 1917. Their company thought they were having a game when they announced they had a ration of raspberries, possibly the only known case of this in the First World War. The enemy was uncooperative over fresh fruit supply during his retreat to the Hindenburg Line early in 1917, felling thousands of fruit trees on their way.

Missing Barrels and Bottles

Tommy removed much wine from cellars, as we saw in the last chapter, but cider was also threatened. Madame tried to refuse accommodation to Major Arthur Behrend's artillery in March 1918 because the cellar was full of cider and potatoes. Behrend had to insist and lectured his gunners about keeping their hands off her produce. Not a spud was taken but the barrels of cider became a bit leaky.

Wine also evaporated from Amiens railway station in October 1918. Lance-Corporal John Jackson and mates, returning to their units from hospital, spotted two enormous barrels of wine on one of the platforms. They attacked them with trenching tools. One burst and they hurriedly filled up their mess tins and water bottles before it all ran away. Also, when they got to the railhead at Bohain they raided a store and stole bread, whole cheeses and pots of jam.

There was a great deal of fuss over a bottle of wine stolen from a brewery in Corbie on 27 June 1916. A corporal was wrongly accused of the deed but his friends found out who the real culprit was. They forced him to come forward with the unopened bottle, not wanting their regiment, the Coldstream Guards, to have its reputation besmirched. The thief was a recruit on his first day in France and had yet to learn about *esprit de corps*.

More Loot

Major Sutherland, CO of 377 Battery, Royal Artillery, actually led a night-time raid on bee hives (4 May 1916). He and his officers were stung but the 'official' report prepared by Lieutenant Carr revealed that although the 'enemy' had been 'buzzing around in enormous numbers' the daring raid had been a sweet success (two dixies of honey).

Some stuff literally fell off the back of lorries. When men of the 17/Leicesters were walking to visit Émilienne at Berles-au-Bois in April 1917, a carcass of mutton fell off an Army Service Corps lorry at their feet. Despite commendable efforts to alert the driver the Leicesters had to admit defeat and were forced to carry it back reluctantly to the company cooks.

It was suggested in many diaries that tins or cartons of jam could open the hearts of young 'mam'selles'. The 2/RWF preferred to sell it at a franc for four tins in April 1915. They were still flogging jam in Béthune a year later, except that the tins actually contained foot grease.

ASC ration dumps were vulnerable to ambitious thieves, such as Dave Barney of the Artists' Rifles. Whilst his pal, Alfred Burrage, was scrounging two plates of food and a loaf to take away from the ASC dump orderlies, Dave was pinching two hams and a lot of bread. Madame at a nearby *estaminet* clasped the hams to her ample breast in ecstasy. She rewarded the enterprising couple with omelettes, containing an incredible number of eggs, red and white wine and packets of chocolate (8 September 1917).

Dumps of fuel also needed closely guarding. The 2/RWF stole a whole dump of coal from a Scots battalion in June 1915.

Hunting and Fishing

In 1916 the multi-talented Fusiliers were hunting water fowl in the reed marshes around Suzanne, mainly by walking down the starving and exhausted birds. Officers were able to do a spot of hunting, especially those of the 2/RWF. Resting at Septmonts in September 1914 they shot pheasants, partridge and rabbits in the woods. On 20 October they found an old pin-fire 12-bore containing twenty rounds. The CO only allowed good shots to participate and supervised the later production of stew. In 1917 they were still hunting, this time at Airaines. On 9 July a local notary invited the CO, Major Poore, to hunt wild boar. The major shot a rabbit and a squirrel. The rabbit was handed to him in a brown paper parcel.

Many soldiers fished; General Maxse's batman fished for hours in the Somme, catching tiddlers in a gauze net on the end of a pole (April 1916) in order to get a plateful for the general's dinner. My father – after his bout of Spanish flu in May 1918 – fished with a stick and a nail in the River Ancre at Avuluy. Before he contracted flu he was digging new trenches in the village of Sylvestre Capel near Hazebrouck, needed because of the threat of the German offensive. He had to help knock down a row of shops, and he and his mates found some expensive goods lying around. George reported this to officers as soon as possible the next day, but not before some of the goods had vanished.

Lieutenant-Colonel Liddell of the 4/Coldstream Guards fished in a small canal at Clairmaris near Poperinghe. He actually did this sitting in the orderly room with a baited stick through an open window. He landed the occasional eel. However, one of his subalterns, Lieutenant Blacker, managed to buy a toy crocodile. It had a compartment in its stomach which Blacker filled with bricks. He attached it to the end of the colonel's line. When the colonel felt this pressure he thought he was about to catch a large one and heaved away, with the result that the crocodile came flying through the window spraying bricks in all directions. The CO, luckily, was highly amused by the prank, a show of toleration which enhanced his reputation as a 'sportsman'.

A popular pastime for Tommy was to throw grenades into rivers, streams and canals in order to stun the fish. The fact that this was punished by twenty-eight days of Field Punishment No. 1 did not deter those angling for a fish dinner. The 1/Hull Pals tried out Mills bombs in the canal in the Nieppe Forest quite near the front line on 21 June 1918. The first detonation – by the signallers – produced ninety-four roach, whereas subsequent bangs by the more 'professional bombers' drew a complete blank. Inevitably, the 2/RWF tried their hand at this game. Two Mills bombs into the La Bassée canal on 29 June 1916 resulted in shoals of floating, unconscious fish.

More conventional tackle brought another Fusilier – fishing with a line from 4am to 9.30pm – not one fish. Another fished for hours without success and finally twigged that someone had tied a carrot to the end of his line. In contrast, the MO of the 8/East Surreys caught a six-pound pike on 21 April 1916 after fishing for fifteen minutes. Rumours that there were oysters in the scum- and corpse-ridden Yser canal were largely discounted and, anyway, there was a lack of bait. Someone suggested cutting up the unpopular padre into small pieces and using him – no offence intended.

Farming

The BEF tried its hand at farming. A Directorate of Agricultural Production was set up late in 1917 with its HQ eventually in Amiens. However, the German offensive in March 1918 upset its plans. Already in existence were modest battalion potato and other vegetable farms along the whole of the British sector covering 7,500 acres. The Directorate was supporting these enterprises with implements, seed and fertilizer. In addition they began to set up their own model farms to demonstrate good practice for the battalion allotments.

There were also poultry farms, a piggery and a slaughter house at Étaples and other base camps; plus a goat farm at Halle aux Blés in Rouen, until the good people of the city complained about the smell, upon which it was moved to Le Granet Quevilly in 2,500 square feet of sheds.

When the Allied counter-offensives got under way in August 1918, agricultural companies moved forward day by day to harvest the wheat, and subsequent fine weather in September and October enabled the Directorate to cut, stack and thatch the crops from over 18,000 acres, and to thresh most of it.

Eighteen

Shops and Restaurants

Separation of Officers and Men

There were shops in quite small villages, not 'domestic shops', but proper establishments on premises designed for business rather than enterprising homes. Restaurants were generally reserved for cities and the bigger towns – and also for officers rather than other ranks. Tommy could not normally afford to eat in them in any case. Mixing between officers and other ranks was frowned on generally. Captain Dunn, the MO of the 2/RWF, saw them mixing in a shop only once during the war, in Le Cateau in August 1914, when circumstances were hardly normal.

Paris

Both officers and men could take leave in Paris. Arthur Osburn, a senior MO, was at the well-known Café de la Paix on 2 September 1914. However, at that time, Paris was still under serious threat from the German Army. So, as Osburn was arriving, the patron was leaving. All he got was an egg. He was very disappointed as he reminisced about the meal he had eaten there in 1910.

V.F. Eberle, an officer in the 2nd Field Company, Royal Engineers, on his way to Italy in November 1917 took tea at Rumpelmayers' Restaurant. Life had long returned to normal in the capital by then, although you still needed to slip someone five francs to ensure you got some breakfast in your hotel. In March 1918 Major Rowland Fielding,

CO of the Connaught Rangers, dined with Prince and Princess Michael Murat, an elaborate and extravagant meal with three different types of wine with each course.

Transport was available to take other ranks from the Gare du Nord to the leave depot. Advice was available on good cafés and cheap hotels, as well as a warning from an MO about the sexual health perils of Paris. Lance-Corporal John Jackson stayed at the Hotel de Malte in September 1918. Food was rationed so he had to pick up ration tickets issued at the depot. He had tea at 'A Corner of Blighty' at No. 20 Place Vendome.

Amiens – Godbert's

Perhaps the most famous restaurant in the northern cities was Godbert's in Amiens. Siegfried Sassoon was there in July 1916 after a stint in Mametz Wood on the Somme. He and other Welsh Fusilier officers dined like dukes in a private room. They ate langoustines, roast duck and drank two bottles of Godbert's best bubbly. They were back there on 1 August. 'Colonel P' was disappointed he didn't get any of the dressed lobster so he got down on all fours and stole a dish of it from another table.

Captain Billy Nevill also favoured Godbert's. He travelled with other officers of the East Surreys in buses from Flixécourt and had a 'ripping' champagne dinner there (20 February 1916). He was back in March and received a warm welcome from Madame Godbert herself. The food was marvellous again and they finished up with a lusty sing-song. Captain J.D. Wyatt of the Gloucestershire Regiment took lunch there in March 1917. His meal consisted of boiled fillet of plaice with lobster and an oyster and mushroom sauce which had won a prize at the Paris Cookery Exhibition. Captain Wyatt and his fellow officers then visited the cinema followed by tea at 'Chat Bleu'.

Siegfried Sassoon was there again in the same month downing two John Collins, one sherry and bitter, one Benedictine, 'Japanese ditto', one oyster cocktail, *pommarel Eilatante* and *trois vernes*. Afterwards he returned to freezing Camp 13. The distance between civilisation and the Western Front was incredibly short. In July 1917 dinner at Godbert's was still the best gastronomic experience behind the lines, although on 28 April of that year Lieutenant Vaughan (1/8/Royal Warwickshires) preferred drinks at the American Bar and a sticky tea at a cake shop.

Godbert's was still offering the same quality on 30 April 1918 when Lieutenant Carr of the 377 Battery, Royal Artillery, was given a lift there by an Australian, who bought him a delicious meal and would not let him pay a penny. Sydney Rogerson ate well at the Hotel du Rhine in Amiens on 20 November 1916, and he also recommended (as well as Godbert's) the Belfort and the Savoy. There was also a spattering of good bars – Aux Huites and Charley's Bar in Rue Corps Nu Sans Teste.

Amiens was good for shopping. Easter 1916 saw Captain Ronald Schweder visiting a sweet shop and buying an Easter egg for his wife. As part of wartime regulations shops were closed between 2pm and 5.30pm – a severe disappointment for V.F. Eberle who stayed in the city in February 1917. Captain Spicer was luckier in January 1918. He wrote home on the 26th praising the quantity and quality of food available in the city. He admitted that it was expensive, but not as pricy as Paris.

Béthune

In August 1915 Béthune had many fine shops and, unlike Armentières, for instance, you didn't need to walk miles from your billet to get there (it was not unusual to have to walk six miles to Armentières and back). Béthune had plenty of billets in and around the town. There was a particularly tasty patisserie with a tremendous range of cakes and candied fruits. Robert Graves considered that Béthune lost its charms later in 1915 when the Canadians arrived. They were able to pay much higher prices, with the result that everybody was charged them. But the fish dinners and cream buns remained a great temptation. Graves thought it had the best cake shop anywhere, including Paris and London, and also a superb hotel (24 June 1915).

Before the Canadians arrived in 1915 Béthune was a culinary treasure trove. In one patisserie there were large, thick flans. The only way that Henry Ogle and his three friends could afford to eat these tasty pastries was to club together to buy one of them. Private John Jackson (6/ Cameronians) was sent to Béthune on 19 August 1915 with eighty francs to buy an assortment of food and drink for his company. He paid far less than Adams later in the year (see below), especially for fresh fruit, clear evidence of the Canadian effect – the price of fresh fruit rocketed up between Jackson's visit and Adams's.

Second Lieutenant Arthur Gibbs complained about the price of fresh fruit. He concluded that shopkeepers in Béthune were taking advantage of a captive market and the fact that some well-to-do officers paid up whatever the cost. Even in a village like Elverdinghe, near Ypres, a little shop near the windmill charged high prices (November 1915). But this place was very near the front line and handy for soldiers looking for something extra in the trenches. Henry Ogle succeeded in getting some Quaker Oats there. Ogle was one of those Tommies who did seem able to frequent shops also used by officers.

In 1917 Private George Adams complained about the one shilling and eight pence asked for a tin of ham (a day's pay for a better-paid private) priced four and a half pence at home – a 450 per cent mark up. There was a similarly exorbitant price for a tin of sardines – a 400 per cent mark up.

On 8 January 1916 Lieutenant L.S. Lloyd (18/Hussars) thought that Béthune was the best French town he had visited: he obviously could afford the prices. He raved about the little pastry shops where you could have afternoon tea. Captain Gore-Browne ate twelve gateaux and drank two pots of tea. This might have been in 'The Globe', a favourite rendez-vous of the Prince of Wales (and Robert Graves). The cakes, the comfort and the service were all first class. It was also the place to have a good sing-song accompanied by a piano player. Lieutenant Spicer remembered it being packed every afternoon in December 1915.

Armentières

Lieutenant Spicer and his fellow officers of the 2/RWF also liked Armentières, despite its distance from the billets. Officers could probably get a lift, anyway. One of them certainly travelled in on a pony because this creature had a daily routine of going up the steps of a café for sugar biscuits (April 1915). Lieutenant Spicer's favourite was a teashop which had been a very high-class patisserie but now attracted a wider clientele to its afternoon teas.

A more serious drawback of Armentières, however, was its proximity to the front line throughout the war (it was captured by the Germans in 1918). Later in 1916 the town became more and more deserted due to frequent shelling. About the only teashop which survived was run by two old ladies. A faded sign – 'Tea Room' – and the equally faded boxes of chocolates in the window were not encouraging. Five shells hit the house in 1916 and the upstairs was ruined. But inside it was very different – bright and cheerful, and very popular with officers because of a pretty girl as much as cakes and tea. William ('Carlos') Carr, an artillery officer with 377 Battery, visited in August 1917. Before joining up he was a hill farmer in Scotland. He became a fine gunnery officer. Despite the battering Armentières regularly suffered he was able to buy ample food and wine to supplement his rations. In September 1917 Armentières got a severe pasting, destroying many of the places where Carr had shopped.

St Omer

St Omer was much further back and a delight at this time. You could buy oranges and tangerines, almost impossible to get in Britain during December 1917. But they were a bit pricy. Tangerines were anything from two and a half pence to four and a half pence each, about the cost of egg and chips in an *estaminet*. Seville oranges were even dearer – three to six pence each. Beetroot sugar was two shillings and five pence for a pound, more than two days' pay for Tommy; butter was two shillings and ten pence a pound. You could have a nice whiting for dinner but it would cost an officer half his day's pay. Some officers ate so well because they had incomes from other sources. Frank Dunham was there on 2 August 1917 and he had fried liver and chips, but from what animal the liver originated was not clear. When he got back to his billet he was violently ill.

St Omer could still boast of 'Le Boeuf', a very high-class restaurant which had moved for obvious reasons from Armentières (there was another one in Rouen). In September 1917 St Omer had many expensive teashops but their supply of cakes was uncertain – they were always coming tomorrow or yesterday.

Poperinghe

The rest town of Poperinghe had some famous restaurants, as well as Talbot House. Second Lieutenant Charles Edmonds (5/Royal Warwickshires) enjoyed 'La Poupée' in September 1917. A bombing raid on the town came on his way back to his billet; it was a dangerous business going to 'La Poupée' – on his previous jaunt there on 29 July, to drink several bottles of champagne with fellow officers, smoke cigars and sip liqueurs, they had been shelled on their way back to bed.

Dinner there in November 1917 set you back four shillings, half a day's pay for an officer. For that there was good soup, whiting (which was dearer to buy fresh in St Omer – how prices ranged), roast chicken and potatoes, cauliflower au gratin, coffee (with as much sugar as you wanted) and bread and butter. There was also a choice of wines at moderate prices.

'Skindles' was also popular; you would see more Flemish people in there. But the officers' favourite was 'Cyril's', more usually known as 'Gingair's' because of the flame-haired, sixteen-year-old, tart-tongued daughter of the house.

Abbéville

Lance-Corporal Henry Ogle visited Abbéville in 1916 and enjoyed fancy cakes, wine and liqueurs, some going for a junior NCO – he must have been getting a steady flow of postal orders. Arthur Behrend, an artillery adjutant, dined at 'Faucond'Or', an old hotel in the main square, in 1915. He remembered the bliss of having a tablecloth on the table, nice knives, forks and spoons and being waited on. A half bottle of Salmon and Gluckstein complemented the meal well and there was still time for the music hall.

Other Towns and Villages

At base camp towns and the ports you could eat well if you had the money. Captain Dunn, MO of the 2/RWF, was in Rouen on 13 August 1914. His several-course meal cost one and a half francs. Prices were set to rise after this. Guy Chapman (13/Royal Fusiliers), returning from a course in Le Havre, stopped off for cocktails in 'The Angleterre' in Rouen in 1916 for a long and tasty lunch, and it cost him a lot more than one and a half francs.

Billy Nevill was at the Hotel Duvaux in Boulogne on 28 July 1915 and the champagne was good. He was in Étaples on 3 March 1916, not out of choice, but because he was stranded after visiting an aunt who was a nurse in the hospital there. A hotel managed an omelette and some veal.

Smaller towns had decent shops and restaurants. The 4/Coldstream Guards discovered numerous well-stocked shops in Estaires early in 1916, where civilian life appeared to be proceeding as usual. John Reith had supper in Bailleul on 21 October 1914 – sardines, omelettes, steak and chips and coffee. Afterwards he visited a little shop and bought boiled sweets and fancy biscuits.

John Glubb, on his way to Arras on 30 March 1917, was delighted to arrive in a town – Querrieu – and see shops and girls after months without a sight of either. One of his men bought him some sweet biscuits amidst a scrum of sappers around a little shop. When he was settled in his billet another man brought him a bottle of wine; he was extremely popular with the men, as you can see. But when the 1/8/ Royal Warwickshires tramped four miles to visit Doullens in the same area on 26 July 1917, all the shops were shut (perhaps because of the afternoon curfew).

Laventie (July 1915) had quite a good hotel and restaurant. The small hotel at St Sylvestre was 'luxurious' according to Guy Chapman. Less glamorous was Major Geiger's experience of table d'hôte in a 'third-rate' restaurant in Le Cateau on 25 August 1914, although this was at a difficult time for civilian restaurateurs.

Quite small villages sometimes had very good shops. One at Gapenner, near Abbéville, was a rich source for Frank Dunham when trying to build up his aid post's own mess in April 1918. He had no trouble getting plenty of good meat and fish, potatoes, eggs, fruit, custard and sweet biscuits, and cooked a very good meal on a 'Princess' stove, not only for his fellow medical team but also a stray dog called Freeze. Sergeant Read (17/Leicesters) fondly remembered the little shop in the village of Bailleulval near Berles-au-Bois for its sweet biscuits, chocolates and candles. It was also an *estaminet*.

Le Cornet Bourdois, near Lillers, remarkably had an oyster bar in a wine shop. It also included an attractive female barber who was the reason for much unnecessary hair-cutting. The Tommy who was looking for a nice pâté in another village shop sadly started eating a large tin of pink metal polish – 'pate'. Surprisingly, he was a teacher in civvy street – obviously not of French.

Nineteen

Drunk and Disorderly or Incapable

A Marvellous Talent for It

According to Lieutenant A.A. Macfarlane Grieve (4/Highland Light Infantry) soldiers at rest got drunk at every opportunity. They had a marvellous talent for it, he reckoned. He may have been referring specifically to the Old Contemptibles. Two men of the 11/Hussars in August 1914 raided an Army warehouse stacked with rum and went on a bender. They were apprehended and sent to prison for three months.

However, men of the New Citizen Armies were also keen on spending a lot of money, energy and time in the pursuit of a drink or two. The obvious place to get intoxicated was an *estaminet*, as wet canteens were not the appropriate place for it, although it was not unknown. Military policemen were thus deputed to keep an eye on *estaminets*, starting from the regular system organised in Vlamertinghe on 16 October 1914. For instance, a substantial police presence was necessary for the 2/RWF plus the Scottish Rifles in the Aisne sector in 1916.

Pay days were particularly critical since some men were prone to blowing the lot on the first night, knocking back laced drinks, such as the Hull Pals on 14 March 1916. This was a good time for fights to break out, such as the brawl connected with the machine-gunners of the 13/Royal Fusiliers near Arras on a night in September 1915, or the one in Contay my father was caught up in. 'Crimes' (offences) ceased to exist amongst the Connaught Rangers in camp at Ervillers in October 1917 because there were no *estaminets* for miles around, only canteens with weak beer.

Parties

Another source of drunken behaviour was the occasional party or event. Dick Richards recalled the tug-o'-war match with the 1/RWF on Whit Sunday 1917. After an enjoyable contest they all retired to the canteen and drank for hours, including some whisky which appeared from somewhere. The boys of the 2nd Battalion, who were playing away, did not reach their billet and slept in a field.

Officers liked parties. There was one in Péronne for the 1/8/Royal Warwickshires on 3 May 1917. Everyone became totally drunk on champagne resulting in a violent rag, during which the enormous and 'disgusting' padre offered to fight six subalterns. After he initially landed one or two telling blows they got him down, took off his trousers and spanked him.

Other ranks did not get a lot of champagne, but Private Read and his mates were introduced to Moet and Chandon in Berles-au-Bois (September 1915) by men of the King's Royal Rifle Corps. On the way back to camp they fell into a ditch. They did get back and then were called on parade, when Read inadvertently threw a parcel at their lieutenant. Luckily, the subaltern turned a blind eye to the fact they were inebriated and Read retired with his parcel hanging above his head in a sandbag. He woke up covered in cake crumbs and bits of sandbag: a rat had eaten the parcel.

Character

Some 'champagne' contained raw spirit at ten francs a bottle, and was lethal. White or red wine fortified with rum was also pretty potent. Other sources of inebriation were the 'treasures' which soldiers discovered in cellars. In Nieuport Bains on 22 June 1917 a small party of the 2/Inniskillin Fusiliers was in charge of a large, sealed store of wine in a cellar. In the morning the 'guards' were all dead drunk. The hoard was then removed but not before those removing it removed some for themselves.

The 'conjuror' of the 2/RWF, whom we met before performing in an *estaminet*, on another occasion was in one in Neuville when he 'found' a supply of cognac. Later he was delivered to the guard room in a wheelbarrow, drunk and beaten up (25 November 1916). Like this character, particular soldiers were well known for being drunk, such as 'Fizzer' Green, also of the 2/RWF. As his nickname indicates, he was often up before the CO on one charge or another connected with drink. In March 1915 the accusation was 'Drunk whilst proceeding to a front line trench'. Fizzer protested that he had given away his rum ration to Private Elliot for the past few weeks. Elliot, according to Fizzer, was prepared to swear on oath that this was the case. Fizzer further explained that he had suffered since a lad with a condition that caused lightning paralysis of the legs, which resulted in him falling over without any warning. The condition was in the family: his uncle had fallen in front of a tram and had been run over. Even the colonel was laughing by this time and Fizzer got away with twenty-eight days Field Punishment No. 1.

Some Tommies acquired the soubriquet of 'Zig-zag', referring to their gait when leaving *estaminets*. Private W.G. Brown was strolling along a lane near St Omer in March 1918 when one such character appeared in front of him. A rather prim French 'mam'selle' found such behaviour unbecoming and declared disdainfully, '*Anglais soldats beaucoup zig-zag tour les jours*'. This was obviously not the same girl addressed by another 'zig-zag' thus: '*Moi, ally au estaminet, revenoir zig-zag, si vous no promenade.*' Whether this cut any ice with the young lady was uncertain.

Some Tommies could not hold their drink. A mess corporal in Estaires on 28 February 1918 was arrested by the military police after apparently drinking only one glass of red wine. Of course, there might have been a little something else in the glass. ASC drivers had more opportunity to take one over the eight. The one bringing up the mail to Poperinghe just before Christmas 1917 went zig-zag with his lorry and strewed the letters and parcels, and himself, all along the Watou road.

Drunk in the Trenches

Being drunk in the trenches was an offence punishable by death, but thankfully this sentence was never carried out, although there was one case where it was touch and go. A group of Scots had drunk a whole jar of rum and destroyed the myth that they never got 'drunk'. Sadly, one of them was a 'barrack-room lawyer' and insisted on pleading guilty and nothing could change his mind. They were in front of a firing squad when the order came through to commute to a prison sentence. The experience probably turned them into teetotallers.

Field punishments were not pleasant – being tied to a wheel or a gate for several hours a day was uncomfortable and demeaning; there was no pay or cigarettes, and bully beef and hard biscuit was issued for every meal. The treatment meted out to a man of the Royal Horse Artillery who had got drunk in March 1916 was worse. The battalion was on the move and he was tied to the back of a wagon. Whenever he fell over he was dragged along the ground until he could stagger upright.

COs often issued the maximum sentence of twenty-eight days of Field Punishment rather than send a man up to a court martial. Three men of the 4/Coldstream Guards on 22 December 1915 were very lucky: not only were they drunk, but it was through drinking whisky, another offence. They only got twenty-eight days. However, if this sort of indiscipline occurred too frequently the lives of other men could be endangered, not to mention the military efforts of the whole battalion. A CO had to draw the line somewhere and bring in a higher author-ity. A drunken man in a forward trench was a serious liability. One in the 13/Royal Fusiliers (September 1917) yelled: 'Over the top! Over the top! We're coming for you!' After the attack was completed an officer searched for this soldier. He found him; he had suffered the worst fate of all. Someone had stuck a bayonet in him, whether friend or foe was not known or no one was saying.

Another sad case concerned the storeman put in charge of a three-gallon jar of rum during the attack on La Bassée (Loos – September 1915). The storeman eventually arrived in the forward trench, red-faced and retching. He collapsed into the mud, dropped the jar and the stopper flew off, allowing what was left in it to dribble out on the duckboards. An officer put one foot on his neck and the other on his back and trod him into the mud. The order to go over the bags was then given.

The 2/RWF were relieving a Cameronian battalion on 19 January 1915 when one of the Scots swayed up on to the parapet but was quickly dragged down. The Scots' CO said to the Fusiliers' CO that his man was not 'drunk' in the Scottish sense of the word. It was not clear what a real Scots drunk would look like – certainly horizontal. Colonel Walter Nicholas described drink as 'an urgent devil', so perhaps a Scot could not be blamed for taking it and so was never 'drunk'. Lieutenant-General Aylmer Hunter-Watson was inspecting trenches when he encountered one such horizontal soldier. 'Dead, sir,' explained a subaltern, whereupon the general saluted. 'I salute the honoured dead,' he intoned. The 'body' peeped out from beneath his blanket and muttered, 'What's the old geezer going on about?' 'Dead drunk, I meant, sir,' the lieutenant added hastily.

Charles Edmonds recalled a whole ration party drunk on the rum for a company. He found them prostrate in a pill box. Some were comatose, the rest cheerful and singing. Edmonds couldn't arrest and send them back because an enemy bombardment was in progress. Actually he felt like roaring with laughter but he gave them a good telling-off, not that many of them comprehended what he was saying or cared. He took back those who could just about move and the others were left to sleep it off. Another ration party (for the 10/Durham Light Infantry) in January 1916 in Elverdinghe was given far too much rum. The result was that the whole company became incoherent before falling fast asleep. NCOs hurriedly took over sentry duty and managed to hide the situation from the officers. Luckily, it was a very quiet front.

There was a tragic event involving two men of the 6/Welch. They managed to drink a whole jar of rum before regurgitating some of it and choking to death. Extra rum was often available when there was a high casualty rate and the normal ration was sent up. This happened to Bernard Livermore. Unfortunately, an officer, thinking he looked frozen, also gave him some whisky. He had not eaten for a day and the result was that he slipped on a wet duckboard and went to sleep. The understanding CSM let him stay there.

Ernest Parker also 'suffered' because he was given too much rum for his section. He resisted the temptation to drink too much but his pals had no such inhibitions and were soon incoherent and flat out, including the sentries. Once again, they had an understanding officer who did not report them.

The case of Private McNaught could have ended tragically. He had also been put in charge of a company's rum supply when the storeman was wounded. When dawn broke an officer became aware that McNaught was lurching about in No Man's Land shouting obscenities at the Germans. But it was New Year's Day 1915 and the Germans were still in a benevolent mood following the Truce. They just laughed and cheered. An officer commanded him to come back. 'Come oot and fetch us,' retorted McNaught, who then slipped and fell back into the trench, to wild applause from across the way.

Drunk and Incapable Officers

Drunk and incapable officers in the trenches created very dangerous situations. Robert Graves was familiar with a company commander who drank two bottles of whisky a day which made him incapable of making proper decisions, causing heavy casualties in his company. If an officer was caught when drunk he was sent straight up for a court martial. Earlier in the war, any officer found guilty of drunkenness in the front line was discharged in ignominy and stripped of his pension, but when conscription came in these men were demoted to privates and sent to another regiment.

Frank Crozier, CO of the 9/Royal Irish Rifles, was well aware that two fellow COs were heavy drinkers and were placing his own battalion in danger. One was so drunk during a handover that the colonel who was supposed to be relieved refused to leave until his fellow CO sobered up. Crozier was as lenient with one of his own company commanders, giving him another chance after he was discovered completely inebriated. George Gaffikin, the offending officer, who was brave and popular, did not offend again.

Some officers were saved by their men when they were the worse for drink. An officer of the 20/Ulster Rifles, on 20 November 1917, the first day of the attack on Cambrai, staggered over the top draped in a green flag, but was rescued by his batman.

The CO of the 17/Leicesters was drunk in Nicholls Redoubt near Arras in August 1916. He lit a Turkish cigarette at night when the enemy trenches were only a few hundred yards away, belching and giving vent to defeatist talk. He said to Corporal Read, who was on HQ guard duty, 'It's our turn to be taken.'

There were many more drunk officers behind the lines, but not normally when they were on duty. The Artists' Rifles – arriving in Le Havre en route for the Arras battlefield in 1917 – had to parade for a resident staff officer. He tottered out of his hut, stared at the assembled Artists for a few seconds and then muttered, 'Y're a dishgrace to your Reg't, whoever you are', and then staggered back into his hut.

Twenty

Officers' Food and Drink

Spartan Food in the Trenches

Trench food for officers could be very unappealing. Siegfried Sassoon, near St Martin Cojuel near Arras on 11 April 1917, had only half a rasher of bacon all day, which he then accidentally dropped into his stove and had to rescue, burning his fingers in the process. John Glubb, on 14 January 1917 in High Wood, Bazentin-le-Petit (Somme), at least had a whole rasher, but it was greasy and he had to eat it off a tin plate. The bread was so frozen he couldn't cut it.

Lieutenant Montague Cleeve, of the Royal Garrison Artillery, in the Somme trenches in July 1916, fried bully beef on a 'bivvy tin' – a tiny saucepan containing a lamp heated by methylated spirit. He thought it was very tasty. Billy Nevill had stewed bully beef and biscuits (23 August 1915). On the 29th his supper was soup and sardines and 'communication trench' bread, *vin* (very) *ordinaire* washed down with a stiff glass of water. Perhaps he needed to raid his flask of brandy after that feast.

On Lieutenant Mottram's first day in the line he had gritty bacon toasted over a candle, dog biscuits, marmalade, butter and tea. He inadvertently drunk the rum ration for six officers. What a way to start! Arthur Osburn had a typical 'dug out dinner' in October 1914. The food wasn't bad, and included 'Buzzard's cakes', but the mud, noise, squalor, fug, drizzle and danger were terrible. Captain Rowland Fielding (3/Coldstream Guards) on 20 October 1916, in the Hohenzollern Redoubt, ate food off the floor as mice ran amongst it.

Breakfast for Lieutenant Sydney Rogerson (2/West Yorkshires) on 11 November 1916 was cold Maconochie, and lunch was cold bully beef. At least he had a drop of whisky. But even neat whisky couldn't compensate for the nauseating beef stew and onions and flies endured by Guy Chapman, nor the rain-soaked bread and cheese and sandbag fibres suffered by Lieutenant Vaughan.

What was Available

Not withstanding the occasional bad meal, officers generally did better than other ranks. It was, after all, what Tommy expected; he accepted social differences. Officers were supposed to have better food and drink. On 3 September 1917 Captain Geoffrey Brown (2/Lancashire Fusiliers) had egg, bacon and tinned sausage for breakfast at 9am. Lunch at 12.30pm was steak, potatoes, beans and a sweet omelette, there was tea, bread and jam at 4pm, and dinner at 8pm was steak, potatoes, tinned fruit and custard. There was nothing unusual about this. It was the sort of food day officers were used to.

For the 7th Field Company, Royal Engineers, on 15 January 1917 (it was very cold in the Somme area) dinner was soup made with powder, meat, potatoes, peas (all out of tins), and milk pudding (puddings alternated with savouries like sardines or ration cheese on toast). Usually the food was not hot and it was always dirty. As Billy Nevill remarked, they got what was available. One of his breakfasts consisted of tinned peaches, sardines, eggs and marmalade – all on the same plate. Later the cook 'mauled' a couple of chickens for dinner.

Officers' mess food was carried about in 'mess boxes' on carts. When the 5/Royal Warwickshires arrived on the Somme in July 1916 all there was in their box was bread and tinned salmon. It came as no surprise that, as they came under enemy shelling at La Boisselle, it was going to be stale bread or hard biscuits and cold bully beef for some time to come.

Mess Subscriptions

Officers were not necessarily going to do all that much better than privates in the rest areas, either in billets or camps. Food and drink in the company messes could be given a boost by extras, paid for by taking subscriptions from all the officers. If this was not the case, with possibly all or nearly all of the officers receiving no income outside of their Army pay, they could not afford substantial subscriptions, especially if they were sending money home to wives and families. Such an ordinary mess might offer stew for lunch and cold bully beef for supper (not dinner) and tea, bread and jam at all meals. They might get some tinned sausage – an item usually denied to Tommy.

Messes a bit higher up the social scale were very different, supported by healthy subscriptions. However, as the war went on, it was less and less likely that you would find messes with many officers who had independent means. The 2/RWF situation was a good example of good sense moderating the desire for a lot of extras. Officers on just five shillings and three pence a day (raised to seven shillings and sixpence in 1915) couldn't afford much and the 2/RWF CO, Colonel Williams, wisely recognised this. At the end of 1914, when many of the old soldiers of the original BEF were gone, he set the mess subscription at only one and a half francs a day (this rose to 2.25 francs in March 1916 and 2.55 francs in September 1916).

Colonel Williams also barred spirits from the mess (apart from the rum ration) in order to take into account the limited subscription rate that was possible. Mind you, this did not mean that all junior officers were scraping the barrel. Second Lieutenant Cyril Rawlings, obviously with social connections and extra income, wrote home extolling Fortnum and Mason's fresh cod roe and preserved ham, chicken in jelly, whole roast duck and rich turtle soup. Of course, he could have finished up eating some of this off boards or shell boxes slammed down in liquid mud (with a tablecloth, of course) or in a rotting tent in pouring rain.

Even someone like Billy Nevill, obviously from a well-to-do family in London, couldn't expect a feast every day. He remembered the fare handed out in billets in September 1915 – lusty hunks of 'timber-wolf' (whatever that was – he had a good turn of phrase) and yellow lumps of soft, fruity material floating in a general 'modicum fluid tasting partially of café-au-lait and tinned Wiltshire sausages'. This was accompanied by ration bread with the 'consistency of a skating rink'. What he missed most was good toast, buckets of coffee, fried lemon sole, haddock, chicken and green vegetables.

Very Decent Meals

However, there were hundreds of examples of good meals eaten in fairly modest messes cooked by ordinary company cooks. The following was the work of John Jackson for officers of the 1/Cameronians in Estaires on 13 April 1918:

> Breakfast – steak, bacon, chips, fried onions, coffee, bread and butter.

> Dinner – roast chicken, boiled potatoes and carrots, rice pudding, coffee and biscuits, wines, cognac and beer.

> Tea – bacon, eggs, tea, cakes and biscuits.

> Supper – coffee, cake, bottled raspberries and cream, glass of rum, punch (night cap).

The rice pudding contained half a pound of butter, as an 'experiment'. One of Jackson's orderlies even went into a field and milked a cow and brought back a pail of fresh milk. It is amazing to think that all this took place during an enemy bombardment.

Officers received better and more frequent parcels than their men. They could go to restaurants and better shops and cafés but they were often eating the same food in the trenches – although Tommy would never get some plump partridge sent up to him like 2/RWF officers received at Polygon Wood on 28 September 1917. In fairness this was followed by fifty-six foodless hours!

Officers were looked after by batmen – or servants. A servant would carry and care for an officer's personal belongings and look to his personal needs – a nice cup of hot cocoa, or Oxo or Bovril on a cold night. Major Eberle's batman saved some plum pudding at Christmas and served it up for him in the following June as a nice surprise.

Tommy had little but scorn for officers who were aloof, austere, uncaring, useless and cowardly. Those with the opposite attributes could expect his devotion and cooperation, such as Charles Edmonds who passed round his spare pack of De Reszkes on 17 July 1916. Frank Dunham's aid post MO shared his whisky, Lieutenant Mottram his 'posset' and Lieutenant Hopkinson his Fortnum and Mason cake.

Whisky and Champagne

Whisky and champagne tended to separate Tommy from his officers although that is not to say he didn't occasionally get hold of some. The cost of 'Old Orkney' (or 'Officers Only' as it was otherwise known) rose steadily throughout the war (more than the average of twenty-five per cent), and by 1917 it would cost a subaltern a day's pay for a bottle of the best (DOM was the best). Black and White could be cheaper and still good, or 'Old Bushmills', or even plain '*vin blanc écossais*' would do if the quality and price were reasonable.

The *BEF Times* of 20 January 1917 announced 'no whisky, no war' following rumours that whisky was 'napoo' – finished. On 12 February, however, it 'took its hat off' to the person who reintroduced the sale of whisky. Robert Graves had a bottle a day by October 1915 to keep himself awake, after never drinking it before and seldom after the war.

Some 'whisky' was foul. An officer in the 15/Londons ordered a product called '9th Hole'. After trying some, he complained to the makers about its quality. They replied rather sharply asking him not to be so offensive, describing the episode as a 'curiosity of war'. The officer wrote again suggesting that '9th Hole' was also a curiosity of the war.

The quality and price of champagne varied greatly. John Glubb paid three francs for a bottle of local stuff in January 1917 in Corbie, a very reasonable price. He must have liked it because he ordered six more bottles to celebrate when he was promoted in March. Siegfried Sassoon, in the same month and the same town, had 'bad' champagne from a wine merchant's house.

Endpiece

The food and drink consumed by the British infantryman on the Western Front varied enormously from place to place and time to time. The diet also varied from man to man serving in the same trench, billet or camp because of rank, frequency and quality of parcels and postal orders and the generosity of pals.

There were good times and bad times for every man – officers and other ranks – in trenches, and generally better times out of them. Everything revolved around surprise; even on the worst days something tasty could turn up, or in a nice billet the rations might not arrive. Very dark days could be livened up with the arrival of a postal order or a cake. An *estaminet* owner might suddenly offer free food and drink for survivors after terrible losses at the front; the meat ration could turn out to be rotten; the canteen could run out of beer or all your pay could disappear in a welter of deductions; you could smell fresh bread and have no money to buy any, but a pal could have a parcel crammed with cigarettes, chocolates and cakes. But whatever the day was like, it was always improved with some tea, rum and fags.

Bibliography

Arthur, Max, *Forgotten Voices of the Great War*, London, 2006

——, *Last Post*, London, 2005

Bairnsfather, Bruce, *Bullets and Billets*, London, 1916

Behrend, Arthur, *As from Kemmel Hill*, London, 1963

Bilton, David, *The Trench: the full story of the 1st Hull Pals*, Barnsley, 2002

Blacker, C.P., *Have you Forgotten London yet?* London, 2000

Bodleian Library, *A Month at the Front: Diary of an Unknown Soldier*, Oxford, 2006

Brophy, John and Partridge, Eric, *Dictionary of Tommies' Songs and Slang 1914–18*, Barnsley, 2008

Brown, Malcolm, *The Imperial War Museum Book of the Western Front*, London, 1993

——, *The Imperial War Museum Book of 1914: the men who went to war*, London, 2004

——, *Tommy Goes to War*, Stroud, 2005

Bruckshaw, Horace, *The Diaries of Pte. Horace Bruckshaw 1915–1916*, London, 1979

Carr, William, *A Time to Leave the Ploughshares: a Gunner Remembers 1917–18*, London, 1985

Carrington, Charles, *Soldier from the War Returning*, Barnsley, 2006

Chapman, Guy, *A Passionate Prodigality*, London, 1985

Chapman, Paul, *A Haven in Hell*, Barnsley, 2000

Coppard, George, *With a Machine Gun to Cambrai*, London, 1980

Corrigan, Gordon, *Mud, Blood and Poppycock*, London, 2003

Downing, W.H., *To the Last Ridge*, London, 1998

Dunham, Frank, *The Long Carry: The Journal of Stretcher Bearer Frank Dunham 1916–18*, Oxford, 1970

Dunn, J.C., *The War the Infantry Knew*, London, 1988

Eberle, V.F., *My Sapper Venture*, London, 1973

Edmonds, Charles, *A Subaltern's War*, London, 1929

'Ex-Private X', *War is War*, London, 1930

Ferguson, Niall, *The Pity of War*, London, 1999

Fielding, Rowland, *War Letters to a Wife*, London, 1929

French, Anthony, *Gone for a Soldier*, Kineton, 1972

Glubb, John, *Into Battle: A Soldier's Diary of the Great War*, London, 1978

Graham, Stephen, *A Private in the Guards,* London, 1928

Graves, Robert, *Goodbye to All That*, London, 2000

Groom, Winston, *A Storm in Flanders: the Ypres Salient 1914–18: Tragedy and Triumph on the Western Front*, London, 2002

Groom, W.H.A., *Poor Bloody Infantry 1914–16: The Truth Untold – a Memoir of the Great War*, London, 1983

Harris, Ruth Elwin, *Billie: the Nevill Letters*, London, 1991

Holmes, Richard, *Tommy: the British Soldier on the Western Front 1914–1918*, London, 2004

In Flanders Fields Museum Guide (Ypres), 2003

Jackson, John, *Private 12768: Memoir of a Tommy*, Stroud, 2005

Lewis, Jon E., *The Mammoth Book of True World War Stories*, London, 2003

McLean, Murray, *Farming and Forestry on the Western Front*, Ipswich, 2004

Mottram, R.H., *Three personal records of the war*, London, 1929

Moynihan, Michael, *Greater Love: letters home 1914–1918*, London, 1980

Ogle, Henry, *The Fateful Battle Line: the Great War Journal and Sketches of Captain Henry Ogle*, London, 1993

Parker, Ernest, *Into Battle: 1914–1918*, London, 1994

Priestley, J.B., *Margin Released*, London, 1962

Read, I.L., *Of Those we Loved*, Edinburgh, 1994

Reid, Walter, *To Arras 1917: A Volunteer's Odyssey*, East Linton, 2003

Reith, John, *Wearing Spurs*, London, 1966

Richards, Frank, *Old Soldiers Never Die*, London, 1933

Rogerson, Sidney, *Twelve Days on the Somme: A Memoir of the Trenches 1916*, London, 2006

Sassoon, Siegfried, *Memoirs of an Infantry Officer*, London, 2000

Simpson, Andy and Donovan, Tom, *Voices from the Trenches: Life and Death on the Western Front*, Stroud, 2006

Slack, Cecil Moorhouse, *Grandfather's Adventures in the Great War, 1914–18*, Ilfracombe, 1977

Spicer, Lancelot Dykes, *Letters from France 1915–1918*, London, 1979

Talbot House, Poperinghe: *Haven in Hell*

Terraine, John, *General Jack's diary: War on the Western Front 1914–1918*, London, 2000

Tyndale-Biscoe, Julian, *Gunner Subaltern: Letters Written by a Young Man to his Father During the Great War*, London, 1971

Van Emden, Richard, *Britain's Last Tommies*, Barnsley, 2005

Vaughan, Edwin Campion, *Some Desperate Glory: The Diary of a Young Officer 1917*, London, 1994

Walsh, Michael, *Brothers in War*, London, 2007

War Office, *Statistics of the Military Effort of the British Empire 1914–1920*

Weeks, George, unpublished memoirs of the Great War

The Wipers Times: The complete series of the famous wartime trench newspaper, London, 2006

Young, Derek, *Scottish Voices from the Great War*, Stroud, 2005

Index